Great Mistakes

of the War

Books by Hanson W. Baldwin

MEN AND SHIPS OF STEEL
(With Wayne Francis Palmer)

THE CAISSONS ROLL

WE SAW IT HAPPEN
Edited, with Shepard Stone

ADMIRAL DEATH

UNITED WE STAND

WHAT THE CITIZEN SHOULD KNOW ABOUT THE NAVY

STRATEGY FOR VICTORY

THE NAVY AT WAR

THE PRICE OF POWER

GREAT MISTAKES OF THE WAR

GREAT MISTAKES
OF THE WAR

BY *Hanson W. Baldwin*

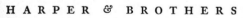

HARPER & BROTHERS
PUBLISHERS · NEW YORK

A somewhat abbreviated version of this book was published in the *Atlantic* in two installments, in the issues of January and February, 1950.

CONTENTS

Great Mistakes

of the War

I. The Basic Fallacy

IN FEBRUARY, 1945, at Yalta, and on June 6, 1944, the
date of the Allied invasion of Normandy, it might be
said that we lost the peace.

American political and strategic mistakes during
the war possibly lengthened it, certainly made it more
difficult, and are largely responsible for the difficulties
and crises through which we have been passing since
the war.

The United States has fought wars differently from
other peoples. We have fought for the immediate victory, not for the ultimate peace. Unlike the British or
the Russians, we have had no grand design, no over-all
concept. This lack of a well-defined political objective to chart our military action has distinguished, to
greater or lesser degree, much of our past history.
During World War II our political mistakes cost us
the peace. The British and the Russians thought and
fought in terms of the big picture, the world after the

war; we thought and fought in terms of what we could do to lick Germany and Japan *now*.

This book is an attempt to illuminate some of these mistakes.

It is, of course, easy to be wise in retrospect and to look back with the benefit of hindsight at the greatest war in history and to point to errors and confusion. They were inevitable, for war is conducted by men and men are fallible. A historian's judgments, moreover, are something like those of a Monday morning global quarterback. Yet if we are ever to learn from our mistakes we must identify them.

The major American wartime errors were all part and parcel of our political immaturity. We fought to win—period. We did not remember that wars are merely an extension of politics by other means; that wars have objectives; that wars without objectives represent particularly senseless slaughters; that unless a nation is to engage in an unlimited holocaust those objectives must be attainable by the available strength, limited by the victor's capacity to enforce them and the willingness of the vanquished state to accept them; and that the general objective of war is a more stable peace. We forgot that the "unity of outlook between allies in war never extends to the subsequent discussion of peace terms." We forgot that "while the attainment of military objectives brings victory in war, it is the attainment of political objectives which wins the subsequent peace."[1] * The United States, in other words, had no peace aims; we had only the vaguest kind of idea, expressed in the vaguest kind of general principles (the Atlantic Charter, the United Nations) of the kind of postwar world we wanted.

Our judgments were emotionally clouded by the perennial American hope for the millenium, the Russian military accomplishments, the warm sense of comradeship with our Allies which the common purpose of victory induced, and by the very single-mindedness of our military-industrial effort. Wartime propaganda added to illusion; all our enemies were knaves, all our Allies friends and comrades—military victory our only purpose. We were, in other words, idealists but not pragmatists. We embarked upon Total War with all the zeal and energy and courage for which Americans are famous, but we fought to win; in the broader sense of an objective, we did not know what we were fighting for.

The political mistakes we made, therefore, sprang from the receptive soil of this immaturity; but they were fertilized, too, by a lack of knowledge or a lack of adequate interpretation of that knowledge. This

* Reference numbers refer to the Notes and Bibliography at the end of the book.

was particularly true of our wartime relationship with Russia. Our policy was founded basically on four great—and false—premises, certainly false in retrospect and seen by some to be false at the time. These were:

1. That the Politburo had abandoned (with the ostensible end of the Communist International) its policy of a world Communist revolution and was honestly interested in the maintenance of friendly relations with capitalist governments.

2. That "Joe" Stalin was a "good fellow" and that we could "get along with him." This was primarily a personal Rooseveltian policy and was based in part upon the judgments formed by Roosevelt as a result of his direct and indirect contacts with Stalin during the war. This belief was shaken in the last months of Roosevelt's life, partly by the Soviet stand on Poland.

3. That Russia might make a separate peace with Germany. Fear of this dominated the waking thoughts of our politico-strategists throughout all the early phases of the war, and some anticipated such an eventuality even after our landing in Normandy.

4. That Russian entry into the war against Japan was either: *a*) essential to victory, or *b*) necessary to save thousands of American lives. Some of our

military men clung to this concept even after the capture of the Marianas and Okinawa.

All of these basic misconceptions, except the second, had one common denominator: lack of adequate knowledge about Russian strengths, purposes, and motivations; and inadequate evaluation and interpretation of the knowledge we did possess, or failure to accept and apply it.

The second mistake could not have been avoided by any amount of knowledge or by the best possible interpretation. The Presidential office, with its vast powers, can, under an executive who is so inclined, formulate a personal foreign policy. This is particularly true in wartime. President Roosevelt liked to transact business—even international business—on a man-to-man basis; he depended heavily upon personal emissaries like Harry Hopkins, and upon his own judgment, and was confident that his estimate of the other fellow was correct. "I just have a hunch," William C. Bullitt quotes Roosevelt as telling him, "that Stalin . . . doesn't want anything but security for his country, and I think that if I give him everything I possibly can and ask nothing from him in return, *noblesse oblige*, he won't try to annex anything and will work with me for a world of democracy and peace."[2]

Had the President been able to lean upon a younger and more vigorous Secretary of State and a stronger State Department he might have depended less upon intuition and snap judgment and more upon careful research and group study. But it was in the character of the man to administer and to govern and to bargain on a "first-name" basis; he relied heavily upon his great persuasive powers and charm, as well as upon his political ego.

A graphic instance of this tendency toward snap decisions and casual dependence upon Stalin's good intentions was provided at Teheran. At that conference, in late 1943, Roosevelt, in one of his tête-à-têtes with Stalin and Churchill, casually agreed, unknown to virtually all of his advisers, that the Russians ought to have one-third of the surrendered Italian fleet. This agreement was put in the form of an oral promise, and Stalin was not one to forget promises.

Our Navy and the British Navy, who were then trying to utilize the surrendered Italian ships—manned by their own crews—to best advantage in Mediterranean convoy and antisubmarine work, knew nothing of this agreement until Russian representatives in Washington asked early in 1944 when they could expect "their share of the Italian Fleet." Navy, State Department, and Joint Chiefs of Staff were dumbfounded; all our efforts had been directed toward enlisting Italian support in the war against Germany; assignment of one-third of the Italian fleet to the Russians as spoils of war would have been a political bombshell which would have handicapped the war effort in the Mediterranean. Accordingly, and to repair the damages of a casual promise made cavalierly without benefit of advice, the Russians were persuaded to accept, in lieu of the Italian vessels, some American and British men-of-war.

This is but one example of Roosevelt's personalized foreign policy—a foreign policy marked more, perhaps, by idealism and altruism than by realism. This Rooseveltian tendency toward international altruism, too often unmoderated by practical politics, seems a strange manifestation in one who domestically was a pragmatic and consummate politician. But it must be remembered that the vision of a "brave new world" was strong in Roosevelt's mind, and his optimistic nature and the great inner wellspring of his faith in man sometimes affected his judgment.

As William L. Langer notes, Roosevelt regarded Russia as the lesser of two evils, and he "shared an idea common at the time that the cult of world revolution was already receding in the minds of the Soviet leaders and they were becoming more and more engrossed in purely national problems."[3] As a result he turned away from the only practical policy that should have governed our actions—opposition to all dictatorships and reliance upon the time-tested balance-of-power policy—to the chimera of so many Americans: a brave new world.

The Presidential ego unavoidably became stronger in Roosevelt's closing years. His great wartime power, the record of victory, the high esteem in which he was held by the world, and the weakness of the State Department all combined to reinforce the President's tendency to depend upon himself. Had the nation then had a National Security Council, or organization for reconciling and presenting military-political views, had it had a strong, well integrated State Department, this personalized foreign policy might have been tempered by riper judgments and more carefully thought out decisions.

One of our greatest weaknesses in the policy field during the war was the failure to equate, evaluate, and integrate military and political policy; there was then no adequate government mechanism, save in the person of the President himself, for such integration.

Former Secretary of War Stimson points out in his book that the formal organization of the Joint Chiefs of Staff had "a most salutary effect [in the military field] on the President's weakness for snap decisions; it thus offset a characteristic which might otherwise have been a serious handicap to his basically sound

strategic instincts."[4] But there was no political coun-
terpart of the Joint Chiefs of Staff; and even if there
had been, it is difficult to conceive that such an organization could have tempered materially the personal
views which Roosevelt formed about Stalin and
Russia.

The other fallacious premises upon which our wartime Russian policy was based, however, could have
been avoided. We became victims of our own propaganda: Russian aims were good and noble, Communism had changed its stripes. A study of Marxian
literature and of the speeches and writings of its high
apostles, Lenin and Stalin, coupled with the expert
knowledge of numerous American specialists, should
have convinced an unbiased mind that international
Communism had not altered its ultimate aim; the wolf
had merely donned a sheep's skin. Had we recognized
this—and all past experience indicates we should have
recognized it—our wartime alliance with Russia
would have been understood for what it clearly was:
a temporary marriage of expediency. In the same manner, a careful study of strategical facts and available
military information should have indicated clearly the
impossibility, *from the Russian point of view*, of a
separate peace with Germany. Such a peace could only
have been bought in the opening years of the war by

major territorial concessions on Russia's part, concessions which might well have imperiled the Stalin
regime, and which, in any case, would have left the
Russo-German conflict in the category of "unfinished
business." In the closing years of the war, when
Russia had everything to gain and nothing to lose by
continuing the struggle to complete victory, a separate
peace would have been politically ludicrous.

There is no doubt whatsoever that it would have
been to the interest of Britain, the United States, and
the world to have allowed—and indeed, to have en-
couraged—the world's two great dictatorships to fight
each other to a frazzle. Such a struggle, with its result-
ant weakening of both Communism and Naziism,
could not but have aided in the establishment of a more
stable peace; it would have placed the democracies in
supreme power in the world, instead of elevating one
totalitarianism at the expense of another and *of the
democracies*. The great opportunity of the democracies for establishing a stable peace came on June 22,
1941, when Germany invaded Russia, but we muffed
the chance. Instead of aiding Russia with supplies and
munitions—but not too much, instead of bombing and
blockading Germany—but not too much, Britain,
joined after Pearl Harbor by the United States, went
all out for "unconditional surrender." We should, in
other words, have occupied the bargaining position

during the war, vis-à-vis Russia. Russia was the invaded power; Russia, fighting a desperate battle on her own soil, was in a death grapple with Germany. We were not similarly threatened. Russia *had* to have our help; we did not, to the same extent, require hers. This misjudgment put us in the role—at times a disgraceful role—of fearful suppliant and propitiating ally, anxious at nearly any cost to keep Russia fighting. As William C. Bullitt put it, "this topsy-turvy world turned upside down, Alice Through the Looking Glass attitude toward the Soviet Union, which our government adopted in the latter part of 1941, was our first step down the road to our present danger."[5]

In retrospect, how stupid! A man being strangled to death struggles with all that's in him; Russia could not quit.

In the same manner, and for much the same reasons, we reversed the policy we should have followed in the Pacific war. Instead of recognizing that Russia, at nearly all costs, would have to participate in that war, if she was to serve her own interests, we "bribed" her to enter it. Port Arthur is written upon the Russian heart; Manchuria has been the locale of Russian expansionist ambitions for nearly a century. Russia had everything to gain and nothing to lose by entering the Pacific war, particularly in 1944 and 1945 when the power of Germany was broken and Japan was beleaguered and in a strategically hopeless position. Yet again we begged and induced, though we, not Russia, occupied the commanding position. We should have tried to keep Russia out of the war against Japan instead of buying her entry.

Edgar Ansel Mowrer, in *The Nightmare of American Foreign Policy*, succinctly summarizes the basic error of our wartime policies: "In winning the war, F. D. R. left nothing to chance. In planning for peace, he bet the future of the American people on one card: that the Soviet Union would prefer peace and collaboration with the West to armed and ideological expansion. He was warned of the risk. He acknowledged the risk. He deliberately took the risk. And he lost."

But the great wartime President shares this responsibility of history with many others. He had many advisers. Most of them, political and military, "bet" on the same "card."

Such were the mistakes of basic policy and principle —most of them stemming from a political immaturity and an international naïveté—which influenced most of our wartime decisions and dominated the nature of the peace. They form the psychological background for many of the mistakes of detail here recounted. But a cautionary and qualifying *caveat* must immediately be entered. Some of these itemized errors were purely fortuitous, the illegitimate offspring of peculiar personalities or specialized circumstance; others were powerfully influenced by American humanitarianism —a desire to save lives; still others were military mistakes, with political connotations—what Bullitt has called "military imagination functioning in political ignorance." But, regardless of their psychological origins, they have one thing in common: they were mistakes.

This is no comprehensive catalogue of error, nor are we concerned here with tactical mistakes or with those military decisions which had no political consequence. These are a selected few of the broad and far-reaching errors which history will supplement, which influenced the course of the war or affected the peace.

II. Germany and Russia—
The Struggle in Europe

1. Unconditional Surrender

THIS was perhaps the biggest political mistake of the war. In the First World War Wilson took care to distinguish between the Kaiser and the militaristic Junkers class and the German people; in the Second, Stalin drew a clear line between Hitler and the Nazis, and the German people, and even the German Army. The opportunity of driving a wedge between rulers and ruled, so clearly seized by Wilson and by Stalin, was muffed by Roosevelt and Churchill. Unconditional surrender was an open invitation to unconditional resistance; it discouraged opposition to Hitler, probably lengthened the war, cost us lives, and helped to lead to the present abortive peace.

This policy grew in part out of the need for a psychological war cry; in part it was intended, as

Langer puts it, as a reassurance to "the Bolshevik leaders that there would be no compromise with Hitler and that the Allies would fight on to total victory."[6] The haunting fear that motivated so many of our actions during the war—the fear of a separate Russian peace with Germany—and Russia's growing suspicions of her Western Allies because of their inability until that time (January, 1943) to open a "second front" on land in Western Europe, dictated the famous declaration of Casablanca.

It is noteworthy that Stalin was never associated with formulating "unconditional surrender" as a doctrine; he refused the invitation to the Casablanca conference, and later specifically criticized this doctrine. Some historians point to the Four Power declaration at Moscow in October, 1943, as an indication of Soviet acceptance of the unconditional surrender policy. Actually, however, this is an oversimplified and inaccurate assessment of the Russian reaction. Prior to and after the Casablanca-Moscow conferences, Stalin took peculiar care to differentiate between the unconditional surrender of Hitlerism, and the unconditional surrender of Germany. Obviously the more complete the German defeat, the greater the extension of Russian power, but Stalin understood well the political advantages of strengthening the anti-Hitler opposition in Germany. In one pronouncement (November 6, 1942) he even promised that a German defeat would not mean the end of "all military force in Germany," and the Soviets took active measures through the Free Germany Committee, the Union of German Officers, and the righ-ranking Germans captured at Stalingrad and elsewhere (Field Marshal von Paulus, Major General Seydlitz, etc.) to back up words with deeds and to build up an active opposition to Hitler.

"This 'soft line' was developed to Germany [by Russia] all through the Summer and Autumn of 1943," Wallace Carroll, who did so much to form our psychological warfare policy during the war, comments. ". . . in November, Stalin challenged the use of the 'hard line' of unconditional surrender at the Teheran Conference."[7] Even as late as May, 1945, when Harry Hopkins was conferring with Stalin in Moscow, Stalin balked at unconditional surrender for Japan, since, "if we stick to [it] . . . the Japs will not give up and we will have to destroy them as we did Germany."[8]

President Roosevelt ignored these challenges to his "hard line" at Teheran, in December, 1943, after the conference, when he was asked by the British in Washington what he was going to do to meet Stalin's objections, and again on later occasions. Despite pressure from the British, the Russians, and strong and repeated demands from Anglo-American military leaders for a definition of unconditional surrender which would strengthen the opposition to Hitler, hasten the end of the war, and provide a positive— instead of a purely negative—war aim, the President never retreated from the Casablanca dictate. His sole concession (in his Christmas Eve speech of 1943) was a pallid reflection, indeed, of the Wilsonian Fourteen Points:

"The United Nations," he said, "have no intention to enslave the German people. We wish them to have a normal chance to develop in peace as useful and respectable members of the European family. But we most certainly emphasize that word, 'respectable,' for we intend to rid them once and for all of Nazism, and Prussian militarism, and the fanatic, disastrous notion that they constitute the 'Master Race.'"

Wallace Carroll defends the doctrine of unconditional surrender in arguments somewhat distinguished by rationalization. But Mr. Carroll himself urged at the time a specific definition of unconditional surrender, and admits that "failure of the Allies to define unconditional surrender was giving Goebbels [even after the Normandy landing] complete freedom to popularize his own version of Allied intentions."[9] Not until December, 1944, with the war almost ended, and using Directive 1067—the directions sent Eisen-

hower for the military government of Germany—
were our propagandists able to indicate to the Germans the hard terms that faced them.

As Langer notes, the Casablanca policy, "far from
scaring the Germans into early surrender . . . gave the
Nazi propagandists their best argument for a last-ditch
resistance.

"On balance it seems that the demand for unconditional surrender was an unfortunate and costly move,
and that it was too high a price to pay for Stalin's
peace of mind."[10]

To this Captain Harry C. Butcher, USNR, lends a
hearty "Amen." He criticizes the "hard-boiled attitude" of the Prime Minister and the President about
unconditional surrender and points out that any "military person knows there are conditions to every
surrender."

"There is a feeling," Butcher notes in his diary, *My
Three Years with Eisenhower*, under entry of April
14, 1944, "that at Casablanca, the President and the
Prime Minister, more likely the former, seized on
Grant's famous term without realizing the full implications to the enemy. Goebbels has made great capital
with it to strengthen the morale of the German Army
and people. . . ."[11]

Butcher was correct; the President was the author
of the famous phrase. Elliott Roosevelt, in his book,

notes that at luncheon on January 23, in his Casablanca villa, attended by Harry Hopkins, Churchill, Roosevelt, and Elliott, the phrase *unconditional surrender* was born: "For what it is worth, it can be recorded that it was Father's phrase, that Harry took an immediate and strong liking to it, and that Churchill, while he slowly munched a mouthful of food, thought, frowned, thought, finally grinned, and at length announced, 'Perfect! And I can see just how Goebbels and the rest of 'em'll squeal!' "[12]

This story of the birth of the famous phrase—endorsed by the President's son, who was present at Casablanca—appears to be an approximate version of what actually occurred. Both Roosevelt and Churchill have agreed that Roosevelt fathered the phrase, and that it was not mentioned publicly until the press conference summarizing the results of the conference. However, it was not a casual inspiration as it has been made to appear, for subsequent events showed it was deeply embedded in Roosevelt's war philosophy and he resisted attempts to modify the doctrine.

Since the war, Mr. Churchill, in a debate in Parliament (July 21, 1949) somewhat disingenuously blamed (or credited?) Roosevelt for the formulation of the unconditional surrender policy, and tried, inferentially, to disassociate himself from it. He stated that at Casablanca President Roosevelt broached the subject "without consultation with me," said it was not his "idea," and admitted that the British Cabinet, had they been consulted, would have rejected the policy. "The first time I heard that phrase used was from the lips of President Roosevelt. . . . I was there on the spot and I had rapidly to consider whether our condition in the world would justify me in not giving support to him."

Mr. Churchill did, however, "give support" to the policy, and still insists that no "great harm" came of it; and thus he cannot escape an inferential share of the blame for what Foreign Secretary Ernest Bevin has excoriated as a policy of anarchy. "Unconditional surrender," Mr. Bevin said in the same debate, "left us a Germany without a law, without a Constitution, and without a single institution to grapple with the problems. . . ."

Mr. Churchill, while damning "unconditional surrender" by a sort of faint praise, admitted in the same debate that at the second Quebec conference he had initialed the Morgenthau "pastoralization" plan for Germany, "about which I do not feel so confident in my conscience about the judgment of my actions."[13]

But on November 17, 1949, in another statement to Parliament, Mr. Churchill corrected his own faulty memory, and substantiated, in general, the account given by Elliott Roosevelt. After consulting the Casablanca conference records, Britain's wartime Prime Minister declared that the words *unconditional surrender* had been mentioned, "probably in informal talk, I think at meal times" on January 19, 1942. Mr. Churchill sent a cable to the British Cabinet informing them that he and President Roosevelt intended to issue an unconditional surrender demand, but to exclude Italy. The Cabinet's response, Mr. Churchill declared, "was not against unconditional surrender.

"They only disagreed with it not being applied to Italy as well."

Strangely enough, however, despite this meeting of the minds between Churchill and Roosevelt and the (at least tacit) approval of the British Cabinet, the official communique of the Casablanca conference did not mention the phrase *unconditional surrender*, and it remained for President Roosevelt to use at a press conference, a phrase that, according to Mr. Churchill, had just popped into his mind.[14]

Roosevelt's debonair use publicly of a phrase that had just "popped into his mind" could not possibly have been the sudden carelessness such a description implies. The evidence is overwhelming that unconditional surrender and its implications were discussed in private at Casablanca prior to public announcement; and Roosevelt was the principal architect of the phrase and of the policy, which was a carefully calculated one.

Regardless of its origins, there is no doubt that it caused grave harm.

B. H. Liddell Hart, the British military writer, found in his postwar interviews with German generals that "but for the unconditional surrender policy, both they and their troops would have yielded sooner, either separately or collectively."[15] The German underground, as noted by Albrecht von Kessel[16] in his diary, felt the unconditional surrender formula greatly handicapped their efforts. In the negotiations leading up to the Italian surrender and collapse, the harsh and strident note of unconditional surrender, modified only slightly and then but temporarily, probably delayed the inevitable collapse of Italy four to six weeks—ample time to permit the reinforcement of the Italian front by the Germans, a reinforcement which was the direct cause of the bloody stalemate that ensued.

Allen W. Dulles' book, *Germany's Underground*,[17] points to the same conclusions. It seems clear that the unconditional surrender policy, plus the policy of indiscriminate bombing, helped to unify Germany and to weaken the anti-Hitler opposition. The doctrine of Casablanca was in direct contradiction to the assurances given by the British Government in public speeches and in private conversations in 1939-40 that a Germany which had rid itself of Hitler and his associates would be an acceptable basis for peace talks. Edward C. W. von Selzem, in a letter to *The New York Times*, points out that the "declaration drove most of the vacillating generals away from the opposition and attached them for better or worse to Hitler, thus weakening detrimentally the cause of the opposition and strengthening considerably Hitler's power of resistance. In this, I contend, the real tragedy of the Casablanca declaration is to be found."[18]

Siegfried Wagener, who served in psychological warfare operations during World War II, in a letter to the author (December 28, 1949) writes that "in the first half of 1944 SHAEF and the Joint Chiefs were approached to foster a German revolution as requested by the then existing German underground." Among the arguments advanced for support of such a revolution, the most important was "getting into the Central European power house before the Russians."

But unconditional surrender, a somewhat naive faith in our ally, and dependence upon military operations for military victory, caused the rejection of the project, "despite a hectic struggle of several months."

The Casablanca conference, with its unconditional surrender doctrine, indicated the Presidential predilection for intuitive decisions and personalized policies—

a fault shared to a considerable degree by Churchill, whose ideas, however, were more fully tempered by a riper wisdom and more seasoned advice. The Casablanca policy came to logical fruition in the Morgenthau "pastoral Germany" policy at Quebec in September, 1944. The outlines of this plan—which fortunately quickly was abandoned—"leaked," and this dire American blueprint for Germany's tomorrow undoubtedly still further stiffened Nazi resistance during the last months of the war.

Unconditional surrender was a policy of political bankruptcy, which delayed our military objective— victory—and confirmed our lack of a reasoned program for peace. It cost us dearly in lives and time, and its essentially negative concept has handicapped the development of a positive peace program.

By endorsing the policy, we abandoned any pragmatic political aims; victory, as defined in these terms, could not possibly mean a more stable peace, for "unconditional surrender" meant, as Liddell Hart has noted, the "complete disappearance of any European balance.

"War to the bitter end was bound to make Russia 'top dog' on the Continent, to leave the countries of Western Europe gravely weakened and to destroy any buffer."[19]

Unconditional surrender could only mean unlimited

war, and unlimited war has never meant—save in the days when Rome sowed the fields of Carthage with salt and destroyed her rival with fire and sword—a more stable peace.

This political policy, coupled with a military policy of promiscuous destruction by strategic bombing, could not help but sow the dragon's teeth of future trouble.

2. Loss of Eastern Europe

The long wartime history of strategic differences between Britain and the United States started soon after Pearl Harbor. From then until just before the invasion of southern France in August, 1944, when the British finally failed in their last effort to persuade us to undertake a Balkan invasion, we steadily championed an invasion of Western Europe and the British consistently proposed an alternative or complementary invasion of the "underbelly."

The two differing strategic concepts were separated, not only by geography and terrain, but by centuries of experience. We sought only military victory—the quickest possible victory. The British looked toward the peace; victory to them had little meaning if it resulted in political losses. We saw in the British insistence upon Southern European "adventures" all sorts of malevolent motives; some of our brash young strategists even claimed the British did not want to fight. It is true that Churchill and his advisers were concerned about saving lives; the blood bath of World War I had weakened Britain dangerously. Churchill was determined to avoid the holocaust of great casualties and long stalemate. As Stimson put it, "the shadows of Passchendaele and Dunkerque still hang too heavily over the imagination of the British."[20] It is also true that to Churchill, victim of the Dardanelles fiasco in World War I, the Balkans were a psychological magnet; victory there in World War II would justify the ill-executed plans of World War I. The great war leader believed in "eccentric" strategy: the utilization of the Allies superior naval and air power to conduct attrition attacks against the enemy's coastlines. The pattern of England's strategy in the Napoleonic wars was in his mind.

These, perhaps, were contributory reasons behind the British strategy. But fundamentally the British evaluation was politico-military; we ignored the first part of that compound word. The British wanted to invade Southern Europe because its lands abut on the Mediterranean and are contiguous to the Near East, important to Britain's power position in the world. For centuries Britain had had major politico-economic interests in Greece, other Balkan states, and Turkey;

for centuries her traditional policy had been to check the expansionism of Russia, to support Turkish control of the Dardanelles, to participate in Danubian riparian rights. In 1942 and 1943, with the Russians in deep retreat and the Germans almost at the Caspian, the British may not have foreseen 1944 and 1945, with the Russians entering the Balkans, but they perceived clearly the political importance of this area, and they saw that an invasion there would preserve it—in the best possible manner, by soldiers on the ground—against either Russian or German interests, and in so doing, would safeguard the British "lifeline" through the Mediterranean. Thus the British believed Germany could be beaten and the peace won "by a series of attritions in northern Italy; in the eastern Mediterranean, in Greece, in the Balkans, in Rumania and other satellite countries."[21]

These proposals were advanced, not only by the British generals, but chiefly and most vigorously by British statesmen—Churchill, Eden, and Smuts. Stimson noted their insistence, yet in his book, *On Active Service*, after citing the factual history of our strategic divergences, he describes as "wholly erroneous" the view that "the British opposition to Overlord [invasion of western France] was guided by a desire to block Soviet Russia by an invasion further east.

"Never in any of his [Stimson's] long and frank

discussions with the British leaders was any such argument advanced, and he saw no need whatever to assume any such grounds for the British position. Not only did the British have many good grounds to fear a cross-Channel undertaking, but Mr. Churchill had been for nearly thirty years a believer in what he called the 'right hook.' In 1943 he retained all his long-held strategic convictions, combined with a natural British concern for the Mediterranean theatre," and in Stimson's view that was all there was to it.[22]

But there was more behind the British position than military logic, Stimson notwithstanding. It is true that the British, in general and except in their most intimate conversations with lower-level Americans than Stimson, utilized military rather than political arguments to bolster their case. But this was natural; Mr. Roosevelt, in some of the discussions, sided with the Russians rather than with Churchill. Moreover, some of our strategic talks were three-cornered; the British could not very well utilize political arguments—the hope of blocking Russia—in conferences which Russian representatives attended; an effort had to be made to maintain the stability of the unnatural "Big Three" alliance that had been created. It must be remembered that during the latter part of the war it was Britain that filled the role the United States now occupies, of chief protagonist vis-à-vis Russia, in the battle for Europe.

Roosevelt was the "mediator," Stalin and Churchill the polite but definite antagonists of the conference tables.

It is, of course, true that British preoccupation with Southern Europe was not wholly political in motive; the British were never stupid enough to think they could win the peace by losing the war. Their military logic was good, although the difficult Balkan terrain did not help their arguments. They believed an invasion through the "soft underbelly" would catch the German Army in the rear, would find a recruitment of strength from the doughty Slavs of the occupied countries, and would provide via the Danube a broad highway into Germany. But the British clearly were thinking of winning the peace as well as the war; observers with less fiery righteousness than Mr. Stimson, but perhaps more perspicacity, noted repeatedly the political-minded mental processes of our allies.

Thus, soon after we entered the war, the British proposed Gymnast (later called Super-Gymnast, and finally Torch)—an invasion of North Africa, at Dakar, Casablanca, the Cape Verdes, or Oran. The original date then mentioned was March, 1942! By January 2, 1942, when General Joseph W. Stilwell, then slated to command Gymnast, attended one of his early conferences in Washington, the lines had been drawn: "Gerow, Somervell, Arnold, Clark, Chief of

Staff, and I. All against it. Limeys claim Spain would 'bitterly oppose' Germans. What rot."[23]

The dispute roared on down the roads of time, exploding now and again at conferences—never settled, always recurrent. The British won the first round; they got the North African invasion, then Sicily and Italy, instead of the plan favored by the Americans: the invasion of western France in July, 1943. But they lost in the end; the growing military power of the United States and the self-assurance of our strategists —sound militarily but weak politically—overbalanced them.

There is no need to trace in detail the fitful fever of this strategical discussion, but a brief chart of these basic differences with our British allies may help the future to understand the errors of the past.

From the time of our entry into the war, and even prior to it, our strategists—Eisenhower, Wedemeyer, Marshall, and Stimson particularly—advocated the defeat of Germany by an invasion of western France. This proposal, as Stimson puts it, was the "brain child of the United States Army."[24]

This invasion was to be timed for 1943; if necessary, to save the Russian front from utter collapse, a small diversionary landing was to be made in France in 1942.

". . . in April, 1942," Admiral King states, "General Marshall had, in consultation with the British in London, taken the initial steps for setting up preparations for an invasion of the continent as the major ultimate step necessary to defeat Germany. It was recognized at that time that it might be necessary to relieve the desperate Russian situation on the Eastern Front by a precipitate landing on the Northern coast of France in late 1942 (Operation Sledgehammer). If Operation Sledgehammer was not found to be necessary the landing was to be undertaken the following Spring, 1943 [Operation Roundup]."[25]

The date for Sledgehammer was originally set for September 15, 1942. The proposed 1943 invasion was given full support by our military leaders. The British were distinctly lukewarm about the project; Churchill was particularly horrified at the thought of the projected 1942 "sacrifice" landing, and from the beginning championed Gymnast, later renamed Torch: the invasion of North Africa. The President initially lent tacit support to the 1943 invasion and, if necessary, to the 1942 diversionary landing, but he was never fully persuaded; and in June, 1942, the whole subject was reopened.

Then, in a famous meeting at the White House, described by Martin Sommers in the *Saturday Evening Post*, Churchill and the American strategists, with Wedemeyer as our spokesman, debated strategy. In this meeting Churchill was eloquent in favor of a

"surge from the Mediterranean along the historic Bel-
grade-Warsaw axis"; Wedemeyer, without the benefit
of the Churchillian rhetoric, spoke logically in favor
of the 1943 cross-Channel operation. As Sommers puts
it, "Churchill, because of his influence on President
Roosevelt, won his fight to avoid a cross-Channel
operation in 1943. He lost on his determination to
force an offensive via Belgrade to Warsaw—*to an
extent because when the Russians heard about this
plan, they raised shrill objections*"[26] (italics mine).

The President, moved in part by his impatience
for action, in part by domestic considerations, insisted upon some American operation in the Euro-
pean-North African theater in 1942, and, as Stimson
puts it, Gymnast, the North African invasion, was the
"President's great secret baby."[27] The President's insistence upon action, plus the course of events—the
Russians, in July, 1942, were fighting with their backs
to the wall at Stalingrad and in the Caucasus—led to
a conference in London in late July, 1942.

"At this conference," writes Admiral King, "the
British Chiefs of Staff were adamant in their view that
the invasion of northern France [Sledgehammer]
could not be undertaken. This view was initially opposed by the United States Chiefs of Staff and the
United States Government. The conference decided,

however, that invasion of French Northwest Africa could and should be undertaken. . . ."[28]

At Casablanca in January, 1943, after the successful invasion of North Africa, the British—to the ill-concealed fury of our strategists—insisted that the cross-Channel operation tentatively scheduled for the spring of 1943 could not possibly be undertaken before the fall, if then.

Churchill and the British were still strong at Casablanca for an attack on the "soft underbelly" of Europe; Churchill saw Sicily as a step toward the Dodecanese Islands, Greece, and the Balkans; "always he was of the opinion that we should contrive our entry into Europe in such a way as to meet the Red Army in central Europe, so that Britain's sphere of influence might be maintained as far east as possible."[29]

But our Allies were also motivated by sound military considerations; in retrospect it is now obvious that our concept of invading Western Europe in 1942 was fantastic; our deficiencies in North Africa, which was a much needed training school for our troops, proved that. The British objection to a 1943 cross-Channel operation was also soundly taken militarily; we would have had in that year neither the trained divisions, the equipment, the planes, the experience, nor (particularly) the landing craft to have invaded the most strongly held part of the continent against an enemy whose strength was far greater than it was a year later.[30]

Sicily inevitably led to an invasion of Italy, an operation envisaged first as a limited one against the boot of the Italian peninsula, then later for the seizure of air bases at Foggia, the quick capture of Rome, and the consequent political-psychological advantage. Churchill saw Italy and Sicily as bases for a jump eastward into the Balkans, and he continued, with the aid of his military leaders, to push this project.

Admiral King points out that although the British specifically agreed to limit the Italian operations and the Mediterranean effort, "they nevertheless as time went on and succeeding conferences took place, continued to press more and more for operations in the Mediterranean and to oppose final and firm commitments for the cross-Channel operation.

"Indeed at Anfa [Casablanca] a number of the British delegation were confident that Germany would accept defeat by January 1, 1944."[31]

But American strength had now been mobilized; Roosevelt was now firm for Overlord (formerly called Roundup), the invasion of Normandy, and the British were forced to agree at Quebec in August, 1943, that Overlord should have the "inside track." While planning and preparations for the cross-Channel operation in late spring of 1944 were being made,

the indefatigable "P. M."—never one to surrender
easily once he had sunk his teeth into an argument—
tried in various ways to modify or postpone Overlord,
or at least to parallel it by an invasion of the Balkans.
He was persistent and insistent, and so were his ad-
visers. Churchill returned to the charge at the Moscow
Conference of Foreign Ministers in October, and at
Cairo and Teheran in late 1943 he made another effort.
At Cairo on November 24 he made a long and elo-
quent talk to the American and British staff and to
Roosevelt about the advantages of operations in the
Aegean Sea and against the island of Rhodes.

At Teheran the British again advocated the Balkan
invasion, but Roosevelt, stressing the geographical advantages of the cross-Channel assault and the terrain
difficulties of the Balkans, said that only an invasion
of western France could be considered, from the Russian point of view a "second front." Stalin naturally
sided with Roosevelt; indeed, the two "got along" not
only at Teheran but at Yalta. The personality of each
attracted the other; the language barrier helped rather
than handicapped the process; Stalin's flattery, but not
Stalin's subtle manipulations, reached the President.
A common tongue, Churchill's great mastery of that
tongue, and his far wider knowledge of the European
world which made his superior political brilliance
perceptible—plus the intransigeant unanimity of

American military advice—made the Stalin-Roosevelt "alliance" possible. As one great witness of those days has put it, "Roosevelt and Stalin were on the same side in any disagreement."[32] And so it was that on November 30, 1943, the invasion of Normandy was finally decided at Teheran, and *Stalin strongly supported the southern France invasion*, rather than a trans-Adriatic operation into the Balkans which was mentioned by Roosevelt and backed strongly by Churchill.

This Teheran decision, in which Stalin's unequivocal insistence upon an invasion of western France and the unanimity of the American military were the decisive factors, really settled the postwar political fate of Eastern Europe.

Major General John R. Deane in his book says of Teheran: "Stalin appeared to know exactly what he wanted at the Conference. This was also true of Churchill, but not so of Roosevelt. This is not said as a reflection on our President, but his apparent indecision was probably the *direct result of our obscure foreign policy*. President Roosevelt was thinking of *winning the war*; the others were thinking of their *relative positions when the war was won*. Stalin wanted the Anglo-American forces in Western not Southern Europe; Churchill thought our postwar position would be improved and British interests best served if the

Anglo-Americans as well as the Russians participated in the occupation of the Balkans."[33] (italics mine)

Even after the definitive decisions of Teheran, Churchill was not quite done; although the Normandy operation was now certain, a companion invasion of the Balkans might be possible.

In Italy, the Allies had been halted in the tangled mountain country south of Rome; the Rapido ran red with blood. Churchill conceived, pushed, and all but executed an amphibious end run. Operation Shingle, the Anzio beachhead landing, was intended to expedite the taking of Rome, and may also have been intended (though this is more doubtful), as Elliott Roosevelt declares, as "Churchill's last—highly individual, resolutely high-handed—attempt to force invasion of Europe via the South rather than the West."[34] But Anzio, too, bogged down, and major American energies were now concentrated on Overlord and Normandy.

Rome fell, and Normandy was invaded, and in the summer of 1944—a summer of Allied triumphs, with the Russian armies still largely in Russia—Churchill made his final efforts to influence the future fate of the world. The British tried repeatedly to have the forces that were to be used in the invasion of southern France committed instead to a cross-Adriatic operation—the objective a landing in the Trieste-Fiume area to take the German armies in Italy on the flank, a push through the Ljubljana Gap into Austria, and a fanning out into the Austro-Hungarian plain with its ideal sites for air bases. By then, Churchill, as he has revealed in private discussions since the war, had no illusions about saving the Balkans from Russian domination; he knew possession, in the Russian lexicon, was nine-tenths of the law; but he did hope that Central Europe could be liberated first by the Western Allies. At a meeting at the headquarters of Field Marshal Sir Henry Maitland Wilson, British supreme commander in the Mediterranean, General Marshall tried to sound out the British and American Mediterranean commanders about the project, which in view of strong British backing was assuming formidable dimensions. General Ira Eaker, then commanding the Mediterranean Air Forces, had not been briefed about General Marshall's antipathy for what he considered an unsound (militarily) diversion, and when asked his opinion in the meeting Eaker said that from the air point of view it would be easier to support a trans-Adriatic operation than the invasion of southern France. The bases, he pointed out, already had been established in Italy, and our planes could operate in support of the Trieste move from these bases. But the southern France operation would have to be supported from new bases in Corsica.

After the meeting was over, General Marshall commented wryly and somewhat bitterly to General Eaker: "You've been too damned long with the British."[35]

In furtherance of their final effort to put Allied troops into Central Europe before the Red Armies occupied those countries, the British "worked" on General Mark W. Clark, then commanding our army in Italy. The King of England, on a visit to the Italian front in July, 1944, about a month before the southern France invasion, is said to have suggested to Clark the advantages of such a Balkan operation and reportedly tried to enlist his support of the project with the Joint Chiefs of Staff.

General Clark, in a letter to this writer, dated October 15, 1948, recalls the King's visit "when we were approaching the Apennines," but adds: "I do not recall that he discussed with me the advisability of pushing our principal effort into the Balkans.

". . . it was common knowledge that the British were desirous of carrying the war into the Balkans. This subject was discussed with me on several occasions by various Britishers in high places, commencing early in 1944. I recall General Alexander [later Field Marshal Viscount Alexander, then in command of all land forces in Italy] presenting his views on this subject. . . . I must say that I agreed with the wisdom of pushing our main effort to the East rather than continue to buck straight ahead against the mountains and the overwhelming resistance of the Germans. To have taken advantage of Tito's situation with the opportunity of landing a part of our forces across the Adriatic, behind protected beachheads which Tito could have provided, with the bulk of our forces in Italy attacking through the Ljubljana Gap would, if successful, have placed the Western Allies in a much stronger position at the end of the war to meet the ever-increasing challenge of Soviet world domination."

In all these discussions of a trans-Adriatic operation, the Ljubljana Gap and the Istrian peninsula were usually favored, but landings further south along the Dalmatian coast near Zara or Split were also mentioned. The British were persistent; the project was pushed "even as late as September, 1944,"[36] after the forces that invaded southern France had formed a junction with Patton's rampaging army that had broken out of the Normandy beachhead.

Much has been made, since the war, of the strategic importance of the southern France invasion; without it, it has been said, most of the German forces south of Brittany would have escaped. But we now know that most of the German forces did escape. The southern France invasion was originally timed to coincide with the invasion of Normandy in June, 1944, and simultaneous invasions in west and south would have divided the German forces in France. But lack of landing craft, caused chiefly by the belated strengthening of the Normandy invasion force, and (to a far lesser extent) the bogging down of the Italian campaign which delayed the amphibious training schedule in the Mediterranean, forced a postponement of the southern France operation until August 15. And we now know from German records that a Nazi withdrawal from France already had started even before the Anvil-Dragoon (southern France) landings. Many German troops were cut up and captured by the junction of Patton's forces with those that landed on the Côte d'Azur, but many of the enemy combat units completed successfully their withdrawal to the German frontier. Much of the strategic meaning of the southern France invasion undoubtedly was lost when the two-months' postponement became necessary; when this decision was reached, the arguments for the trans-Adriatic invasion became overwhelming.

Despite these arguments it was not to be; the British, despite the great eloquence of Churchill and the reasoned logic of his staff, had failed; the American strategy—heartily endorsed by the Russians—was the pattern of conquest.

It was, of course, a successful pattern, for it was a very sound plan militarily, probably sounder in a military sense than a Balkan invasion, and it led to unconditional surrender. But it also led to the domination of Eastern and Central Europe by Russia and the postwar upset in the European balance of power which has been so obvious since the war. American strategy was not, of course, the only factor in this political defeat. Churchill made his share of mistakes. Initially, he embraced the Russians, when the Germans attacked them, like a band of brothers. His—and our—abandonment of Mikhailovitch in Yugoslavia and his endorsement of Tito (formalized at Teheran), whom he thought he could control with British gold; the tacit acceptance of Russia's claims to Poland's eastern territories and the division of Europe into spheres of influence with predominant control of the Balkans—except for Greece and Yugoslavia—allotted to Russia, also contributed to our loss of the peace. This latter was a particularly heinous mistake. Churchill was its principal architect. He recognized, apparently as early as 1942, Russia's "predominant interest" in Eastern Europe. Secretary Hull opposed this concept, but the President, without Hull's knowledge, agreed to the initial arrangement. Further agreements between London and Moscow in 1944, *coupled with the concentration of Western military strength in France, instead of Southern and Central Europe*, further fortified the Russian position.

But the dominant factor in the political complexion of Europe after the war was the presence of Red Army soldiers in all the countries east of the Trieste-Stettin line. The eruption of the Russians into the Danube basin gave them control over one of Europe's greatest waterways, access to Central Europe's granaries and great cities, and a strategical position of tremendous power at the center of Europe.

An invasion of Southern Europe might have avoided this unfortunate climax to a war of "liberation." Champions of the western invasion point out that attack from the south might have permitted the Russians to advance through northern Germany, almost unchecked, to the Low Countries, and perhaps even into France. This seems highly unlikely. In the north the Nazis fought in defense of their own soil; in the south, of alien soil. The bitter last-ditch German defense on the Oder and the bloody battle of Berlin showed the type of fanatic resistance the Reichswehr offered in the north; in the Balkans, on the other hand, resistance was sporadic. A large-scale Mediterranean invasion might have been mounted some months sooner than the June, 1944, attack in Normandy; bases already were available in North Africa, Sicily, and Italy, and the dirty Channel winter weather was not a factor. There was a real chance, as Churchill believed, that a push from Belgrade up the Danube into Czechoslovakia, eastern Germany, and perhaps into Poland would have beaten the Red Armies to northern Europe.

A southern invasion, in any case, presupposed a war of limited military objectives and definite political aims, not unconditional surrender or unlimited conquest. It implied a beaten Germany but also a weakened Russia.

And attack through the "soft underbelly" and invasion from the west were never mutually exclusive operations. One naturally complemented the other; this was particularly true after the successful invasion of Normandy. There can be little argument that the invasion of southern France two months after the Normandy attack had little military, and no political, significance; our main effort in the Mediterranean should have been transferred from France and Italy across the Adriatic.

All of this Churchill and the British had clearly foreseen; none of this, insofar as the public record goes, did we foresee. Not *all* Americans, of course, were so completely bereft of political foresight. But those who possessed it were not in positions of power. A paper was actually written in the old Military Intelligence Division (G-2) of the War Department warning of the exact dangers which later developed. But the authors had their ears pinned back by a superior, who told them sharply: "The Russians have no political objectives in the Balkans; they are there for military reasons only."

The majority of Americans who had the power to influence events opposed the British concept of invasion of Europe through the "underbelly." Yet, so great was our physical strength, so impeccable our military logic, that rationalization triumphed over foresight. Today some of the principal architects of our policy understand their mistakes; and many of our great military figures of the war now admit freely that the British were right and we were wrong. For we forgot that all wars have objectives and all victories conditions; we forgot that winning the peace is equally as important as winning the war; we forgot that politico-military is a compound word.

3. LOSS OF CENTRAL EUROPE

Just as our problems in Eastern Europe had their roots in the political astigmatism of Teheran, so our postwar difficulties and defeats in Central Europe— notably in Berlin and Vienna and Czechoslovakia— are the fruit of mistakes made during the war in discussions in Washington and London, Quebec, and Yalta.

The Soviet ground blockade of Berlin, which brought the United States so close to war with Russia in 1948, was possible only because the United States had no control over the communications to Berlin, and no precise written definition of our communication rights. The postwar Communist coup in Czechoslovakia was aided by Russian propaganda, which pointed out that Prague had been liberated by Russian arms. In Austria, too, the Russians made good postwar political capital of their wartime accomplishments. These difficulties stem directly from our lack of politico-military realism during the war.

Our failure to define properly our right of access to Berlin has been placed publicly almost exclusively on the shoulders of a dead man—the late John G. Winant, wartime Ambassador to Britain, and the chief U. S. representative on the European Advisory Commission. This commission, composed of representatives of the United States, Great Britain, and Russia, commenced after the Teheran conference in December, 1943 (where Roosevelt, Churchill, and Stalin briefly discussed the subject of postwar Germany) to consider the German problem, including the problems of occupation and government and the geographical limitations of the zones to be occupied by the various Allies.

Winant was a sincere idealist, who hoped for the

"brave new world." He was devoted to his country's interests and to the welfare of man, but as an Ambassador he was somewhat vague and his administration was more distinguished for its impulsive warmth than its precision.

One of the Ambassador's very good friends, who had flown with him during the first war and who held a high command during the second war, told this writer that it was his understanding that Mr. Winant resisted military attempts to define precisely our control of the corridor to Berlin, and declared: ". . . the Russians are our Allies and we must trust them, must have faith in them. If you don't have faith you have nothing. . . ." Such a remark *seems* in character.

Nevertheless, this writer is convinced that the blame for Berlin cannot be laid—exclusively, or even to a major degree—upon the shoulders of Winant. One who knew his work well in the European Advisory Commission has written: "Mr. Winant's basic position was that our most difficult and dangerous postwar problem would be our relations [and Britain's] with Russia; that it was important to secure as wide a measure of written agreement as possible during hostilities since our direct bargaining power would decline rapidly after the end of hostilities; that America was in the strongest position to press for such agreements; that the agreements should be so detailed and precise that the Russians could not quibble out of them; and that we must deal frankly and fully with the Russians. . . . Mr. Winant was neither 'a trusting soul' nor an 'appeaser.' "

The truth is that the old and dangerous dichotomy between foreign and military policies seems to have been, in part, responsible for the lack of definition of a Berlin approach corridor. Winant, and the U. S. delegation to the European Advisory Commission, did not really make policy; they had a certain amount of freedom and initiative, but all major instructions were the product of Washington, and emanated primarily from the President and the Secretaries of War and State.

Coordination between the military and the State departments in Washington was supposed to have been accomplished by the Working Security Committee, the predecessor of the State-War-Navy Coordinating Committee (the famous SWINK), and the conclusions of this committee were approved by the Joint Chiefs of Staff and the Secretary of State, and, in major issues, by Roosevelt. Minor instructions to the European Advisory Commission were often cleared by the Working Security Committee with an Assistant Secretary of State or an individual member of the Joint Chiefs of Staff. All agreements reached in the EAC were formally approved by the Joint Chiefs of

Staff, by the Secretary of State, and by the President, and only then was Mr. Winant permitted to write letters to the other heads of delegations confirming the agreements signed. Mr. Winant, therefore, was an agent rather than a formulator; the blame, as in most of our wartime mistakes, rests primarily upon Washington.

When the European Advisory Commission was meeting in its first months of life (December, 1943, and January, 1944), the State Department proposed in Washington that the three zones of postwar occupation in Germany (France had not then been included as an occupying power) be so drawn as to bring each into contact with Berlin. For some reason that defies logical understanding now, the War Department rejected this suggestion, which would have solved nearly all our postwar Berlin difficulties, so that it was never even broached in the EAC. In February, 1944, the British informally suggested that a "corridor" to Berlin be established and defined, but the War Department again objected, stating that this was not a subject for the European Advisory Commission, but that the entire question of access to Berlin was "a military matter" which should be settled at the proper time by military representatives.

This eventually was the solution, but the military representatives made a botch of it. In May, 1945, our

armies stood deep on German soil. The zonal occupation agreements for Germany, worked out by the
EAC, approved at the Quebec conference, and modified at Yalta (to include France) placed Berlin in the
Russian zone; the British and U. S. zonal boundaries—
contrary to the original recommendation of the State
Department—lay 100 miles to the west. In May, 1945,
EAC's work was done, and SHAEF was briefed as to
its accomplishments.

The SHAEF representative inquired about access
to Berlin and was told by the European Advisory
Commission that this problem had been left by War
Department insistence to the military, and that with
U. S. troops already fighting in what eventually was
scheduled to become part of the Russian zone of occupation of Germany, the whole question of withdrawal of our troops from the Russian zone and access
to Berlin ought to be taken up together. In other
words, even as late as May, 1945, at the war's end, we
still had a bargaining point; we were in possession—
by conquest—of large parts of Germany, including
areas slated to be in the Russian zone; we could have
conditioned our withdrawal upon acceptance by the
Russians of a secure access corridor to our zone in
Berlin. The SHAEF representative, in fact, was told
that such a corridor agreement ought to include the
establishment of our own guard, with U. S. troops

along the access road and railroad, establishment of vehicle repair and supply points, military telegraph and telephone, right to repair and maintain the road and railroads, and provision for definite alternative routes in case the named routes were not usable for any reason.

This advice was not heeded. The military themselves, after the German collapse, in an agreement of June, 1945, concluded an arrangement which was so general and imprecise as to be productive of future trouble. General Lucius D. Clay has assumed responsibility for the terms of this agreement, and he must bear part of this burden, but he alone is not responsible. The advice he received was none too good; the dangerous breach between State and War still existed; and Eisenhower, Clay, and their advisers negotiated against the background of a psychological delusion, then so prevalent in our government, that the Russians were our political as well as military "buddies," and that we could "get along" with Stalin. But basically and fundamentally the responsibility for the Berlin corridor fiasco rests with the War Department in Washington; at the time the European Advisory Commission was conducting negotiations, the War Department, working with a weak State Department, had the bit in its teeth and assumed a mantle it had neither

competence nor right to wear: the mantle of divine
political wisdom.

In retrospect, it seems probable that the War Department's triumph in this interdepartment struggle
for power in Washington was foreordained. The War
Department's senior personnel were stronger and
more able men; they had behind them, in war, the
great force of public backing. The die—which was
to be indicative of later decisions—was probably cast
early in the war, when Robert Murphy, who was to
be the State Department's and Roosevelt's political
representative in North Africa, was made political
adviser, subordinate to General Eisenhower, instead
of an Ambassador autonomous in his own right.

It was thus largely on the basis of "faith"—faith
not alone in the Russians, but military faith in the
military interpretation of political problems—that the
Berlin corridor agreement was drawn up.

But the corridor agreement was not only the product of this mistake, not only the by-product of the
interdepartment struggle for power in Washington.

In March and April, 1945, as the war against Germany was drawing to an end, Eastern Europe had
gone irretrievably; our earlier failure to invade the
Balkans had cost us dearly. But important parts of
central Europe—Berlin, the Bohemian bastion, and
Prague, and possibly Vienna—were still at stake.

As early as March 28, with the Allied armies on the Rhine three hundred miles from Berlin and the Russians on the Oder thirty miles from Berlin, General Eisenhower sent a personal message to Stalin via the U. S. Military Mission in Moscow. This message outlined his plans for a strong push in the center by General Omar Bradley's American forces to a junction with the Russians on the Elbe, to be followed by flank drives by the British in the north to cut off the Danish peninsula and seize the North German ports, and by the Americans and French in the south into Austria to eliminate the possibility of a last-ditch stand by the Nazis in the so-called "National Redoubt." Churchill protested this communication by Eisenhower to Stalin as an intrusion by the military into political matters, and was vehemently critical of the plan; in Eisenhower's words, "he was greatly disappointed and disturbed because my plan did not first throw Montgomery forward with all the strength I could give him from the American forces in the desperate attempt to capture Berlin before the Russians could do so."[37] But Churchill's protest to Washington was overruled.

Eisenhower's defense against this protest has some merits; there is no doubt that he was perfectly within his rights in communicating his plans to Stalin; he had been previously authorized to do so. But his dismissal of the Berlin plan as militarily unwise, and his fear that an attempt to take the city would necessitate diversion

of forces from other parts of the front to that sole
task—a "stupid" diversion—and his overemphasis on
the "National Redoubt" were, it is now clear, mistaken. Intelligence failures again played a part in this
mistake; the "National Redoubt"—fortifications and
supplies supposed to have been prepared by the Nazi
SS formations in the German-Austrian Alps for a last
stand—was grossly overrated in our estimates. We
learned later that relatively little work on the "Redoubt" had been done; the scheme was more an idea
than an accomplishment. Churchill, in other words,
again emerges in the Berlin matter a wily old fox of
international politics; his vision was not obscured by
the needs of the moment.

Our troops, after crossing the Rhine, swept eastward with relatively little opposition. Agreements had
been reached with the Russians that when contact
between the two armies seemed imminent, a line of
demarcation should be arranged beyond which each
army should not move. This boundary was "temporarily fixed"—in the words of General Eisenhower's
final report—"in the central sector" along the easily
identified line of the Elbe and Mulde rivers; the Russians were so notified in Eisenhower's message to
Stalin of March 28 (which evoked the Churchill protest). By April 12, the first American bridgehead
across the Elbe had been established; we were 100

miles from Berlin, and the Russians, thirty miles from that city on the Oder, were just starting their final offensive. It was not until April 25 that the Russians reached the Elbe; in other words, for about three weeks our forces remained virtually static on that line of demarcation, and not until early May was the Russian battle for Berlin finally won.

Further south our troops moved into Czechoslovakia on April 18, and then on to Pilsen. Prague lay virtually defenseless near at hand; reconnaissance elements of the Third Army were in its outskirts. The Soviet High Command, when informed by General Eisenhower that our troops would move on toward Prague if (in former Secretary of State Byrne's words) "the situation required it,"[38] requested that our forces "should not advance beyond the Budejovice-Pilsen-Karlsbad line." So again our troops marked time, and the honor and political prestige of taking Prague went to the Russians. "I was very much chagrined," noted the late General George S. Patton, Jr., "because I felt, and I still feel, that we should have gone on to the Moldau River and if the Russians didn't like it, let them go to hell."[39]

So, too, in the south, where the agreed demarcation line ran down the Budejovice-Linz railroad and along the valley of the Enns, Vienna, a possible prize, was voluntarily relinquished.

There was some military reason for this restraint. Two armies surging forward toward each other—a desperate enemy in between—are difficult to control; Eisenhower was concerned about accidental collisions. Moreover, it would not have been easy for us to take Berlin first. The Russians were thirty miles from that city when we were a hundred miles away on the Elbe; and though General Omar N. Bradley estimated that we could take the city, or at least participate in its capture, it would be at the cost of perhaps 100,000 casualties. Our troops had been moving fast and hard; the supply problem was difficult—and in any case the Western Allies had advanced far beyond the zonal boundaries agreed upon by the Allied governments, and further advance would only have meant eventual evacuation of additional territory east of the Elbe.

Eisenhower felt moreover (in his own words in his final report) that "Berlin no longer represented a military objective of major importance" and that "military factors, when the enemy was on the brink of final defeat, were more important . . . than the political considerations involved in an Allied capture of the capital."

General Eisenhower's own inclinations about Berlin apparently had the full support of Washington; Edgar Ansel Mowrer reports in *The Nightmare of American Foreign Policy* that he had been personally told by the White House that "the Joint Chiefs of Staff advised Truman to let the Russians take Berlin." President Truman, new to the White House and without much background about the past nuances of our politico-military policies, apparently acceded.

Both political and military decisions, therefore, halted our armies along the Elbe, the Mulde, and the Enns in the closing days of the Third Reich. There *were* military reasons, which seemed good at the time, for not pressing the advance to the utmost, but they were not decisive; the boundaries marked out by the European Advisory Commission and approved at Quebec and Yalta colored the thinking of our commanders. We *could* have moved further eastward. But the political die had been cast; there was not much point in military sacrifice for a political lost cause.

The effect of all these decisions was to make Berlin an island in a Russian sea and to give Soviet troops firm control of Central Europe.

III. *Japan and Russia—*
The Struggle in the Pacific

THE GREAT American military mistakes of the war, which may be said to have cost us the peace, were all part and parcel of our political immaturity. We fought to win—period. We gave far too little thought to the victory of the peace.

In the war against Germany, some of our outstanding political-strategic mistakes, from the point of view of winning the peace, were our failure to invade the Balkans, unconditional surrender, and the errors which led to the loss of Central Europe, which were described in the first part of this book. But the war against Germany had no monopoly of errors; we erred also in the Pacific. We won the war against Japan, but who will say—against the background of the Orient of today—that we won the peace?

The political mistakes made in the war against

Japan were several and major; this discussion is not a catalogue of them all, but merely a notation on a few of them.

One of the greatest of these errors—our failure to develop a politically viable China policy—is treated only inferentially in these pages under the section "Appeasement in Asia." The importance of this failure is now patent; as these words are written the Chinese Communist armies have stormed to the gateways to Southeast Asia, the crumbling remnants of the Chiang Kai-shek regime are broken and scattered, and Communism has won on the Asiatic continent a campaign of vast implications.

The mistakes of Yalta, described in the second part of this book, illuminate and are the fundamental background for the errors in our China policy.

Those errors were founded on the same philosophical quicksand that betrayed our steps in Europe. We could "play ball" with the Chinese Communists, it was said. An influential school of American politicians, diplomats, and generals hewed to this idea, even up to the abortive end of General George C. Marshall's impossible mission to China after the war, when he was given the task of reconciling the irreconcilable: of merging Communism with the Chiang Kai-shek government. We forgot again in China that true cooperation with militant Communism is impossible, except on Communism's own terms, and that the Chinese Communists were no less an enemy of ours than they had been during the war, of Japan.

But we made other grievous errors in China which compounded the basic one.

One was a mistake in personnel. General Joseph W. Stilwell was a lovable character, and a fine soldier; but his sometimes acidulous frankness, epitomized by his nickname "Vinegar Joe," the difficulty he had in working with the British, and his natural tendency to give primacy to military, rather than political, considerations did not make him the ideal theater commander in the most difficult theater of the war, one where toughness needed to be combined with urbanity and with great political *savoir-faire*. Major General Claire L. Chennault, Air Commander in China, was proficient and effective at his calling—although he, in common with many air commanders, underestimated air strengths required and tended to neglect ground strengths—but he carried on a disgraceful feud with Stilwell, his superior, was at times almost insubordinate, and his arrogant egoism made him, at best, difficult.

Myths of our own creation accounted for other basic mistakes. We saw China through an emotional cloud, made up of one part missionary propaganda; one part the Chinaman of legend, complete with bound feet, bird's-nest soup, and pigtail; and one part subjective concepts. We thought—erroneously—of China in terms of a nation, and of the Chinese Government in terms of Western governments; hence the shock and disillusionment were greater than they need have been when the corruption, dictatorial methods, and brutality of the Chiang Kai-shek regime—practices common to China and to most Chinese governments for decades—became known. We were sold a bill of goods about the Chinese Communists; we were told they were merely "agrarian reformers," Chinese first and Communists second. (We heard the same thing in Czechoslovakia after the war, and Benes and Masaryk paid for this mistake with their lives.) And, above all, we were idealistic but not pragmatic; we helped the Chinese generously but not wisely, not selectively. We evolved—painfully, slowly, and with difficulty—control over the supplies we gave during the war, but no sooner was military victory won than we dissolved, voluntarily, our wartime supply system, and we relinquished all real control over events in China. And yet throughout the war and the chaotic period of civil war that followed we could have called the tune; the Chiang Kai-shek government needed us far more than we needed it.

To trace the tangled skein of these mistakes in China through the war years is beyond the scope of this book; only the basic error, epitomized by Yalta, is treated here. But it should never be forgotten that our errors of omission and commission were manifold in China; here, as in so many other theaters, we lost the battles for the peace.

1. MacArthur and the Philippines—Origins of Service Jealousies

The defense of the Philippines was an epic of stout-hearted suffering, but it was marred by differences, frictions, and discords—and high-level errors—which influenced the course of the war in the Pacific. Mac-Arthur, who created around himself the legend of a military demigod, was the focus of some of these troubles; others stemmed from our failure to equate military policies with political policies in the Philippines.

Out of the first Philippine campaign stemmed some of the friction which later divided the Army and Navy in the Pacific. The origin of this friction, in part, predates the war. MacArthur, and the stiff-necked old sea dog then commanding our Asiatic fleet, Admiral Thomas C. Hart, were markedly dissimilar personalities; each had strong and differing ideas, and they did not entirely "get along." This feeling was transmitted to subordinates and pervaded the upper echelons of the two commands.

The situation was worsened by the successful Japanese attack *nine hours after the assault on Pearl Harbor* on our grounded bombers at Clark airfield. In the aftermath of recriminations, published since the war, the Air Force inferentially has blamed the Army, and the Army the Air Force, for this debacle.

It is clear that there were misconceptions on both sides; as former Secretary of War Stimson points out, "it was quickly apparent that the hopes of the previous autumn could not be realized; there would be no successful defense of the Philippines by air power. The preparations had not been completed; the Japanese were too strong; most important of all, there had been no adequate realization of the degree to which air power is dependent on other things than unsupported airplanes. . . . Thus the defense of the Philippines became once more the desperate and losing struggle which had been forecast in the planning of earlier years."[40]

This misconception, a major one, was only partially shared by the Navy, which had not believed the "hopes of the previous autumn" possible of fulfillment without absolute control of the sea and the supply lines to the Philippines, something we could not insure even before Pearl Harbor. The Navy, along with the Army and Air Force, however, had underestimated Japanese strength and had based much of its planning on the assumption that the battleship was still queen of the seas.

Admiral Frederick C. Sherman comments, "our naval high command at that time little realized that control of the sea was dependent on the air power of carriers and not upon the obsolete battleships which were put out of action at Pearl Harbor. . . .

"What rendered the Japanese carrier attack on Pearl Harbor a justifiable risk, from the enemy viewpoint, was the fact that at the opening of the war they had ten carriers to our seven, of which we had only three in the Pacific. This disparity was the main factor in forcing us to take the defensive in the early part of the war, and not the loss of our battleships, as popularly believed."[41] Our underestimation of the Japanese, which stemmed from the highest quarters, was major.

At a background secret press conference in the War Department, seven Washington correspondents were told by a top-ranking Army official on November 15, 1941, that we were on the brink of war with Japan, that our position was *highly favorable* in that our strength in the Philippines was far larger than the Japanese imagined, and that we were preparing not only to defend the Philippines but to conduct an aerial offensive from those islands against Japan. We had, the War Department authority said, *thirty-five* Flying Fortresses in the Philippines—*the greatest concentration of heavy bomber strength anywhere in the world.* More planes were being sent, so were tanks and guns; the Philippines were being reinforced daily. If war did start, the B-17's would be dispatched immediately to set the "paper" cities of Japan on fire and to attack the enemy's naval bases. The B-17's, he admitted, did not have quite enough range to make the round trip from the Philippines to Japan and return, but they could continue to Vladivostok, said the Army official optimistically, and if we got into war we would expect to have such an arrangement with the Russians. (Even before war we thus incorrectly assessed Russia's willingness to cooperate.) The new B-24's would soon be coming off the production lines, the correspondents were told, and the Japanese had no pursuit planes that could reach these high-flying bombers! By about December 15, the War Department would feel rather secure in the Philippines. Flying weather over Japan was propitious; our high-flying bombers could quickly wreak havoc. If a Pacific war started, there would not be much need for our Navy; the U. S. bombers could do the trick virtually single-handed, or, to paraphrase the spokesman's words, without the use of our shipping!

Our own Pacific fleet would stay out of range of
Japanese air power in Hawaii.*

This profound catalogue of error shows not only
how bemused our top strategists had become with
the enthusiastic but misguided tenets of the apostles
of airpower, but it demonstrates graphically how
little we knew about Japan and Japanese strength.

It also points to a dangerous dichotomy in our
strategy. In January, February, and March, 1941, almost a year before we entered the war, "staff conversations between representatives of the Army and Navy
of Great Britain and the United States took place in
Washington."[42] "Rainbow Five," the basic war plan
of the United States, was the ultimate result. It represented the revision and distillation of many previous
plans; it was "world-wide in its provisions," "called for
a defensive strategy in the Pacific and Far East," and
"accepted implicitly the loss of the Philippines, Guam,
and Wake."[43] It was "completed not long before the

* The postwar reasons given for these mistaken judgments are
interesting. A group of planes, which was to "reenforce heavily"
the few Flying Fortresses in the Philippines were delayed for
some weeks by adverse winds and bad weather. Our 1941 appre-
ciation of what air power meant, of what it could do and what
it could not do, was deficient. We did not understand that air
power included airfields, antiaircraft guns, and ground troops for
the protection of those fields, all grossly deficient in the Philippines.
Our judgments of what air power could do were also grossly
exaggerated. The range of the B-17 was considerably overestimated.
The Air Force ability to bomb shipping from high altitudes was
greatly overestimated.

Japanese attack on Pearl Harbor in December, 1941."[44]

Rainbow Five specifically stated that "if Japan does enter the war, the military strategy in the Far East will be defensive," and added that "the United States does not intend to add to its present military strength"[45] in the area. . . .

But a later revision (November, 1941) provided for "offensive air operations in furtherance of the strategic defensive. . . ."[46]

Rainbow Five was complicated by the existence of two other plans, as Dr. Louis Morton, of the Historical Division of the Army, points out in his forthcoming official history *The Fall of the Philippines*. The Orange plan "was based on the assumption that only the United States and Japan would be at war. . . . it held out no promise of immediate reenforcement to the Philippine garrison, but stated that the Navy, in a series of operations, would move westward across the Pacific as rapidly as possible, while maintaining secure its line of communications." Both Rainbow Five and Orange envisaged Philippine defense as confined to the area around Manila Bay, specifically Bataan and Corregidor.

But a third plan, that of the Philippine Commonwealth, developed by General MacArthur (then the military adviser) contemplated a defense of the entire archipelago, although it was not scheduled to go into effect until 1946, when the Philippines acquired their independence.[47]

Thus, in the fall of 1941, at the very time war was imminent, three discordant plans for the defense of the Philippines existed, "no single one of which was followed in its entirety when war came."[48] Army and Air Force leaders were talking—in Washington—in terms of an air offensive against Japan, based on the Philippines; troops, planes, tanks, and guns were being rushed to the Philippines and the Western Pacific in a belated reversal of prior planning; and a mistaken confidence in the defensibility of the islands mounted.

These last-minute and drastic revisions in our Philippine strategic concepts were due in considerable part to the dangerous gap that existed between our military and political policies, in part to the influence in Washington of the air power enthusiasts, and in part to MacArthur, whose prewar estimates of his ability to defend the Philippines were wildly overoptimistic.

MacArthur put a ridiculously high value—as records in future volumes of the Army's official history will show—in the Philippine motor torpedo boat "Navy," with which he hoped to repel Japanese landing attempts. There were only about two Philippine MTB's available when war started, and they played a negative role. MacArthur's prewar assessment of the combat value of the Philippine Army, composed largely of five-and-a-half-month drafted men, was far higher than was warranted, and his mobilization and training schedule apparently was predicated on a belief that hostilities probably would not start until April 1, 1942. Moreover, he seemed to feel that the "alert" message sent to him about November 27, 1941, by the War Department, which indicated war was coming and that the first overt act should be committed by Japan, compelled him to await attack *in the Philippines* (despite the prior attack on Pearl Harbor) before he could undertake the offensive air action contemplated by Rainbow War Plan #5.

The Navy, in common with the Army and Air Force, did not anticipate "the rapidity and strength"[49] of the Japanese offensive. Yet throughout the war, the Navy—personified by the stubborn, able, "sundowner" Admiral Ernest J. King—pressed continuously, usually against some opposition from the Army (which was focusing its attention primarily on Europe), for greater strength in the Pacific.

The history of those days clearly reveals that there need not have been, despite these dangerous divisions and basic misconceptions, such rapid destruction of our Philippine bombing squadrons.

The Air Force had planned, if war came, to utilize

its bombers (about half based on Luzon, half on Mindanao) in reconnoitering and attacking Japanese bases in Formosa; at least twice on the morning of December 8 (December 7, Pearl Harbor time) it requested MacArthur's permission, through his Chief of Staff, aggressive, egotistic, but able Major General Richard K. Sutherland, to launch the attack. Had permission been given, no great results could have been anticipated; our strength was too small, our inexperience considerable, and we possessed little accurate information about target objectives. In other words, the Air Force planning lacked comprehensiveness.

But it would have been far better to have utilized our bombers in an offensive mission than to allow them to be caught, like sitting ducks, in a "strictly defensive" attitude on the ground.[50] MacArthur has never made a comprehensive explanation about this defeat, but he has stated that no recommendation from Lieutenant General (then Major General) L. H. Brereton, then our air commander in the Philippines, to bomb Formosa ever was received, and that he knew "nothing of such a recommendation having been made." General MacArthur added—a strange comment for a commander who knew that the best defense was attack and who knew the defensive-offensive projected by Rainbow Five—that "the over-all strategic mission of the Philippine command was to defend the Philippines, not to initiate an outside [*sic*] attack." He continued: "Our air forces in the Philippines were hardly more than a token force . . . hopelessly outnumbered . . . never had a chance of winning. The date of April 1 . . . was the earliest possible date for the arrival of the necessary reenforcements which would make a successful defense of the Philippines possible."[51]

(These statements stand in strong contrast to the optimistic prewar reports of General MacArthur, and indicate a change of opinion on his part after hostilities commenced.)

General Sutherland, MacArthur's Chief of Staff, who took much upon himself, may have taken the responsibility of refusing permission for the Formosa raid, though he blames Brereton. The Sutherland statement is, however, partially refuted by an entry in the "Summary of Activities, Headquarters Far East Air Force" under 9 A.M., December 8 (Philippine time), six hours after Pearl Harbor: "In response to query from General Brereton a message received from General Sutherland advising planes not authorized to carry bombs at this time."[52] But regardless of Sutherland's actions, MacArthur has revealed since the war that a request to bomb Formosa, had it reached him, probably would have met delay. An attack on Formosa with the small American force available would have had little chance of success, he said.

The postwar statements by General MacArthur reveal either a considerable gulf between the War Department's concept of Far East strategy as revealed in the press conference of November 15 and Mac-Arthur's defensive concept of that time, or a change of mind on MacArthur's part since the war.

MacArthur's then dual status as Field Marshal in the Philippine Army and General in the American Army, his belief—a mistaken one, as the war showed—that the Philippines could, in large measure, provide their own defense, and the American commitment to Philippine independence, seem to have influenced his judgment. Faced with an actual act of war—the Japanese attack upon Pearl Harbor some hours previously—he hesitated, apparently, to undertake offensive action while awaiting either an enemy overt act against the Philippines or formalization of hostilities by actual declaration.

This compounded friction; to the Army-Navy difficulties was now added friction with the Air Force.

These difficulties grew—as indeed they were bound to in any losing action—during the Bataan fighting and the siege of Corregidor. Friction that should have been minimized was, however, maximized by MacArthur's own mistakes.

His communiques bore so little resemblance to actual events that when the gist of them, cast in a cheerful mood of utter unreality, was broadcast, via U. S. radio, to our suffering troops on Bataan, they aroused actual resentment. This error was compounded on January 15, when, in a personal message from MacArthur, his troops were told that "help is on the way from the United States. Thousands of troops and hundreds of planes are being dispatched. The exact time of arrival of reenforcements is unknown. . . ."

Hopes of some were raised briefly by this utterly fantastic order; but it was an ultimate depressant, for its promises could never be kept.

MacArthur's own example did little to inspire his men. He rarely visited Bataan; it was on Corregidor that he got the name "Dugout Doug." This appellation —an utterly unfair one, in which the Navy delighted —cast unwarranted reflections on MacArthur's personal courage, which is outstanding. Time and again in two world wars, MacArthur has demonstrated a calm and exemplary bravery. The fact remains that on the Philippines he was aloof from his troops and rarely left "The Rock"; not until months later, in New Guinea, when his staff began to note the need for such visits, did he commence to circulate among his men.

Contrary to the instructions previously issued to

his subordinates, MacArthur had kept his family in Manila when all other service families had been ordered home; Mrs. MacArthur, his son, and his son's nurse were with the General on Corregidor and took the place of men who might have escaped when the General on orders from Washington left "The Rock" on March 11.

During his stay on Corregidor, MacArthur left many details to his chief of staff, General Sutherland, and there was, among the Marines who served on Corregidor and Bataan, a well confirmed suspicion that the high command did not like Marines. For weeks there was no mention in communiques or press releases of the Marines; finally, when a radio from Corregidor casually named them, the Navy Department had to assure the people of the United States that the Fourth Regiment of Marines had been in the Philippines all along, and that this belated mention did not mean the fleet had broken through the Japanese blockade and had landed reinforcements. Two days before MacArthur left for Australia, the general recommended *all* units on Bataan and Corregidor, *with the exception of Marine and naval units*, for unit citations. Sutherland let it be known that this was no oversight; the Marines had gotten their share of glory in World War I, and they weren't going to get any in this one! Wainwright, who succeeded MacArthur in command, rectified this egregious error as soon as he took over, but the damage had been done; fuel was added to the fire of Army-Navy friction, and the MacArthur mistakes of the first Philippine campaign —mistakes of personality and judgment—overshadowed the relationships between the services throughout the rest of the war.

But the most amazing and the least understandable of MacArthur's Philippine actions was his tacit approval of a proposal by President Quezon on February 8, 1942, that the Philippines "receive immediate and unconditional independence from the United States, and that they be forthwith neutralized by agreement between Japan and the United States; all troops were to be withdrawn and the Philippine Army disbanded." The message from Quezon to President Roosevelt railed against the United States for its failure to reinforce the Philippines "in terms as unfair as they were wholly understandable." What was not understandable was the tacit approval of MacArthur, demigod in his own image, hero of Bataan in the eyes of the world. MacArthur radioed the President that "so far as the military angle is concerned, the problem presents itself as to whether the plan of President Quezon might offer the best possible solution of what is about to be a disastrous debacle."[53] This, just twenty-four days after promising his men that thousands of reinforcements and hundreds of planes were on the way!

MacArthur saw advantages, regardless of whether or not the Japanese accepted the plan; he failed to understand the terrible damage that would have been done, not alone to his own reputation, but above all to American arms and the American purpose, that even the public broaching of such a suggestion would have meant. Bataan, in those days and in those times, had become the symbol of that purpose; amidst defeat we sought heroes and found them in the battered "bastards of Bataan." With one stroke of a pen Mac-Arthur would have wrecked all this forever, and would have left a people confused, bewildered, and resentful about what undoubtedly would have meant a "moral abdication." Such would have been the psychological consequences of any such act; the proposal in any case was so utterly unrealistic—depending as it did upon Japanese stupidity or Japanese benevolence, neither a noted enemy characteristic—as to be absurd.

Fortunately, wiser heads in Washington rejected emphatically this suggestion and directed that "American forces will continue to keep our flag flying in the Philippines so long as there remains any possibility of resistance."[54]

The first Philippine campaign was not, therefore,

solely an epic of tragic glory; feuds and frictions and mistakes left behind an aftermath of bitterness and recrimination that persisted throughout the Pacific war.

But the worst defeat American arms ever have suffered need never have been entered in the history books had we reconciled our military and political policies prior to the war. Dr. Morton has put it well: . "The planning for the defense of the Philippine Islands shows clearly the dilemma in which the United States found itself. National policy dictated the defense of an insular possession, which, in the best opinion of American military advisers, could not be defended with existing naval and military forces. Plans were made for the defense of the Philippines, but these plans were based on conditions which few of the responsible planners believed could be fulfilled."[55]

2. APPEASEMENT IN ASIA

Perhaps the saddest chapter in the long history of political futility which the war recorded was the Yalta conference of February, 1945. As former Secretary of War Stimson writes, "much of the policy of the United States toward Russia, from Teheran to Potsdam, was dominated by the eagerness of the

Americans to secure a firm Russian commitment to enter the Pacific war."[56] This "eagerness" was first manifest at Teheran when Russia's need for warm-water ports was discussed and Roosevelt suggested the establishment of Dairen in Manchuria as an international free port.[57] It reached its crescendo at Yalta, where we attempted to pin down prior elusive Soviet promises to take up arms against Japan. The negotiations about future action against the Japanese were interspersed with discussions of the peace settlement and the German question in Europe, and their political implications were made secondary to the President's prime objective at Yalta—"the brave new world," the establishment of the basic framework of the United Nations.

For all these reasons—and because of a fundamental military as well as political misconception—Russia held the whip hand, and U. S. representatives placed themselves in the amazing position of "giving away" territories which did not belong to us, and of undertaking to secure concessions which impaired the sovereignty of a friendly allied state. The political misconception, so obvious now, should have been apparent then; it was not to our interest, or the interests of China or of the world, to make Russia a Pacific power; it was not to our interest to beg or barter for Russia's entry into the Pacific war.

Nor should military considerations have affected this political judgment. At the time of Yalta, Japan was already beaten—not by the atomic bomb, which had not yet been perfected, not by conventional bombing, then just starting, but by attrition and blockade. The home islands were severed from the empire by our conquest of the Philippines and the Marianas, and the submarine and surface blockade already had brought the pinch of hunger and the stress of severe raw material shortages to Japan. Even before the first bomb was dropped by our B-29's on the Japanese home islands, the enemy aircraft industry was disrupted and on the decline; shortages due to the blockade and a chaotic program of decentralization, dispersion, and underground development, badly carried out, already had reduced severely the output of Japanese factories. The full seriousness of the Japanese plight was not then, of course, completely understood. Our military men were preoccupied and concerned with the fierceness of the Japanese defense; the tactical situation obscured the hopeless strategic position of Japan, and some of our commanders took, therefore, far too pessimistic a view. Mistakes in intelligence, or rather in evaluation, also contributed to an erroneous assessment of Japanese intentions and capabilities. We feared that even after the main Japanese islands had been conquered, the enemy resistance would continue on the continent of Asia with the much-vaunted Kwan-tung Manchurian Army as its core. Yet our intelligence officers in Washington and throughout the Pacific for months had been identifying units of the Kwantung Army and of its air support which had been transferred from that quiet area to various battle sectors.

By late 1944 it was—or should have been—apparent that what remained of the Kwantung Army was largely composed of green conscripts and second-rate troops, with virtually no air support, incapable of a prolonged campaign; it had been bled white to provide reinforcements for other fronts. We also confused Japanese capabilities with Japanese intentions. We believed the Japanese would resist to the last man, no matter how hopelessly beaten.

These beliefs, which were completely erroneous, influenced materially the politico-military approach made at Yalta. They were not held, at the time, by all our experts; but they were, unfortunately, the controlling opinions. Prior to the conference, an intelligence estimate of the Japanese strength had been furnished to the Joint Chiefs of Staff. This estimate, which served as the basis of their judgments at Yalta, was extremely pessimistic; it estimated that there were at least 700,000 men in the Kwantung Army (and a total of 2,000,000 on the Asiatic mainland) and that they were first-rate troops, well trained and well armed. Without Russian assistance, it was estimated, the Japanese might be able to prolong the war on the Japanese mainland (even after the main islands of Japan had been conquered) until the fall of 1946 or even until 1947 or 1948.[58] Other intelligence estimates, notably a far more optimistic one prepared by different authors in the intelligence section of the War Department General Staff, and one naval estimate challenged this viewpoint. So did two intelligence papers which were prepared for the Combined Chiefs of Staff (Anglo-American) in September, 1944, and January, 1945. These papers stated that Japanese shipping and naval and air forces had been broken, and their whole tone seemed to indicate (though they did not explicitly so state) that Japan was on its last legs. Best available information indicates the more realistic estimates never reached Joint Chiefs of Staff level,[59] although Admiral William D. Leahy, the Presidential chief of staff, may have seen the naval estimate.

These more realistic intelligence estimates, which never reached the top echelon at Yalta, were based on numerous factual reports which were available at the time, and which have been verified by postwar investigations. Thus, Lieutenant General Ija Kawabe, commander of the Japanese Air Army in Manchuria from May, 1943, to August, 1944, told interrogators of the Strategic Bombing Survey that "in July or August of 1943 the bulk of [his] planes were moved out of Manchuria. . . .

"For the last six months I was there, anyhow, the actual planes which could be considered operational were nil—practically none."[60]

After the Yalta conference had convened, still another intelligence estimate, prepared by the Twentieth Air Force, was sent to Yalta. This estimate took the viewpoint that the bombardment and blockade of the Japanese main islands had had serious effect and that Japanese resistance was rapidly weakening. This estimate, too, never reached the highest echelons. Thus, the Joint Chiefs of Staff, who gave Roosevelt the military advice upon which his political decisions were (in part) based, framed their own judgments at Yalta on the basis of a faulty intelligence estimate.

General Marshall was then convinced that an invasion of the Japanese main islands was essential, and he insisted that help from Russia on the mainland of Asia was necessary. Admiral King seemed to share this view. But there were divergences of opinion as to the necessity of this operation; Admiral William D. Leahy, who feared the cost in casualties of invasion and who correctly assessed the crippling effect of the blockade on Japan, opposed the invasion. The compromise eventually reached—a sensible one—was to prepare for invasion but in the meantime to utilize the blockade and air bombardment to the utmost to bring Japan to her knees.

These strategic differences—and a failure to appreciate fully the hopeless strategical position of Japan—colored the military thinking at Yalta and helped to lead to indefensible political arrangements. "Certainly," as the *Washington Post* has commented, "the Chiefs of Staff made a blunder to advise Roosevelt and Churchill at Yalta that Japan would last 18 months after V-E Day. Our military men underrated Japan at the beginning of the war, then overrated it, and refused to see the patent fact, obvious to the Navy, that Japan was through even while the brass hats were meeting at Yalta."[61]

Yet at Yalta—and even at the Potsdam conference in July, 1945, when Hitler lay dead and dishonored near the ruins of his bunker in Berlin, and the Third Reich was broken and shattered—one month before the surrender of Japan, there were still many Americans who were interested primarily in getting a firm commitment from Russia to enter the Pacific war.

This mistaken policy stemmed in part from the basic political misconceptions outlined at the beginning of this book, in part from strategic misconceptions, some of them based on inadequate logistical planning. As General Deane points out in his book, our planners were obsessed with two ideas: to bring Russia into the Pacific war, and to utilize Russian territory as bases for our war effort against Japan. Repeatedly, General Deane and other U. S. representatives had pressed Soviet leaders, long before Yalta, for permission to utilize Russian territory as air bases for our attacks on Japan.[62] Yet the cart was put before the horse: We made diplomatic representations for this permission before we had estimated, logistically, the value of such bases to us.

Our attempts to get firm Soviet commitments about the war against Japan reached a preliminary crisis in October, 1944 (more than four months before Yalta), when Churchill and a British entourage visited Moscow. General Deane describes the resulting conferences which he attended as the principal American military representative.[63] Stalin reiterated his intention, first announced to Cordell Hull at Moscow in *October, 1943*, then more or less formalized at Teheran, of entering the Pacific war; said he needed three months after V-E Day to stockpile supplies in Siberia, declared that the U. S. could have air bases and one naval base in the Far East; but added that "if the United States and Great Britain preferred to bring Japan to her knees without Russian participation, he was ready to agree." Furthermore, there was a little item of additional supplies that Russia would require to help her build up a two months' reserve in Siberia. All in all, Stalin said, the Russians would need more than 1,000,000 tons of cargo, and they must be delivered by June 30, 1945, the deliveries to be in addition to those already being made under the Fourth Lend-Lease Protocol. In Moscow, in 1944, Stalin made many glowing promises, but, "despite these promises, the end result was that the Russians got their supplies and the United States got nothing except a belated and last-minute Russian attack against the Japanese."[64]

As the Soviets stalled on their promises and we delivered supplies, the months drew on into the winter of 1944-45; and at Yalta, in February, President Roosevelt, pressed by the U. S. Chiefs of Staff, again took up the questions of bomber bases in Siberia and the date of Russian entry into the Pacific war. Stalin again agreed in principle and set the date at three months after victory in Europe had been won. He said the U. S. could establish bases in the Komsomolsk-Nikolaevsk area and eventually in Kamchatka. But he got down in black and white his price: the Curzon line for the eastern border of Poland, the Kurile Islands, and controlling economic and strategic concessions in Manchuria. (Stalin's Manchurian "price" for Russia's entry into the Pacific war had first been broached, apparently with no grave objections on our part, at

Teheran in December, 1943, just a few days after Roosevelt, Churchill, and Chiang Kai-shek had agreed in the Cairo Declaration that Manchuria and Formosa should be restored to China.)

But it was not until the spring, when Germany was at her last gasp and Japan near the end, that, in the words of General Deane *"it was found that the net increase that would result from putting four groups of B-29's in the Amur River district would be 1.39 per cent of the total bomb tonnage we could place on Japan without using Russian bases"* (italics mine). This was convincing proof, adds Deane, "that the slight increase in our bombing effort and the advantage of an added direction of approach for our bomber formations were not at all commensurate with the logistical effort involved in establishing our forces in Siberia."[65]

A little late—after more than three years of U. S. participation in the war and numerous major concessions to Russia, concessions which were to affect the peace—to be making this ABC logistical discovery! By then Russia had most of the supplies she had demanded; and she had carefully recorded the secret concessions of Yalta.

Russia drove a hard bargain at Yalta. Stalin promised to enter the war against Japan within an estimated ninety days after the end of the war against Germany, but for it he got the Kurile Islands,[66] all of Sakhalin, half-interest in the railways in Manchuria, Port Arthur, a Russian-controlled "free port" in Dairen, and thus strategic hegemony in important northeast Asia.

". . . it is my belief," writes Sherwood, "that Roosevelt would not have agreed to that final firm commitment had it not been that the Yalta Conference was almost at an end and he was tired and anxious to avoid further argument. I believe that he was hopeful that when the time came to notify the Chinese, he would be able to straighten the whole thing out with Chiang Kai-shek—but that hope, of course, was not realized."[67]

These agreements were made with no representative of China, the country most affected by them, present; we undertook the amazing task of helping to secure Chinese acquiescence in arrangements which in effect gave away Chinese territory and advanced the border of Communist Russia almost to Peiping. Nor did we do this gently. The Chinese ratified the Yalta agreements under pressure from the United States, or as the recently issued China White Paper ("United States Relations with China") explains it: "The American view is that the Yalta agreement shall be complied with—no more, no less."[68]

The fault was doubly grievous. We not only hurt our own interests and those of a friendly ally, but at Yalta—inferentially, at least—we broke our pledged word to that ally. For at Cairo in 1943, before the Teheran conference and after Stalin had told Hull in Moscow that Russia would enter the Pacific war, we promised publicly the restoration of Manchuria to China. And to a pragmatic politician, Russian control of Port Arthur and a half interest in the Manchurian railways could only mean Soviet strategic hegemony over Manchuria.

Nor was this all. During the discussions, it was suggested by President Roosevelt that perhaps the Russians ought to have a commercial outlet to the Persian Gulf; and maybe the Trans-Iranian railway, built by American engineers with the help of American capital, ought to be partially owned by Russia, or at least Russia should have certain transit rights! Fortunately wiser counsel soft-pedaled the proposal, and Stalin, apparently suspicious, showed no interest.

No wonder Stimson wrote that the meeting at Yalta dealt "a good deal in altruism and idealism instead of stark realities."[69]

3. THE ATOMIC BOMB—
THE PENALTY OF EXPEDIENCY

The utilization of the atomic bomb against a prostrate and defeated Japan in the closing days of the war exemplifies—even more graphically than any of the mistakes previously recounted—the narrow, astigmatic concentration of our planners upon one goal, and one alone: victory.

Nowhere in all of Mr. Stimson's forceful and eloquent apologia for the leveling of Hiroshima and Nagasaki is there any evidence of an ulterior vision; indeed, the entire effort of his famous Harper's article, reprinted and rearranged in his book, *On Active Service* is focused on proving that the bomb hastened the end of the war. But at what cost!

To accept the Stimson thesis that the atomic bomb should have been used as it was used, it is necessary first to accept the contention that the atomic bomb achieved or hastened victory, and second, and more important, that it helped to consolidate the peace or to further the political aims for which war was fought.

History can accept neither contention.

Let us examine the first. The atomic bomb was dropped in August. Long before that month started our forces were securely based in Okinawa, the Marianas and Iwo Jima; Germany had been defeated; our fleet had been cruising off the Japanese coast with impunity bombarding the shoreline; our submarines were operating in the Sea of Japan; even inter-island ferries had been attacked and sunk. Bombing, which started slowly in June, 1944, from China bases and from the Marianas in November, 1944, had been increased materially in 1945, and by August, 1945, more than 16,000 tons of bombs had ravaged Japanese cities. Food was short; mines and submarines and surface vessels and planes clamped an iron blockade around the main islands; raw materials were scarce. Blockade, bombing, and unsuccessful attempts at dispersion had reduced Japanese production capacity from 20 to 60 per cent. The enemy, in a military sense, was in a hopeless strategic position by the time the Potsdam demand for unconditional surrender was made on July 26.

Such, then, was the situation when we wiped out Hiroshima and Nagasaki.

Need we have done it? No one can, of course, be positive, but the answer is almost certainly negative.

The invasion of Japan, which Admiral Leahy had opposed as too wasteful of American blood, and in any case unnecessary, was scheduled (for the southern island of Kyushu) for Nov. 1, 1945, to be followed if necessary, in the spring of 1946, by a major landing on the main island of Honshu. We dropped the two atomic bombs in early August, almost two months before our first D-Day. The decision to drop them, after the Japanese rejection of the Potsdam ultimatum, was a pretty hasty one. It followed the recommendations of Secretary Stimson and an "Interim Committee" of distinguished officials and scientists, who had found "no acceptable alternative to direct military use."[70]

But the weakness of this statement is inherent, for none was tried and "military use" of the bomb was undertaken despite strong opposition to this course by numerous scientists and Japanese experts, including former Ambassador Joseph Grew. Not only was the Potsdam ultimatum merely a restatement of the politically impossible—unconditional surrender—but it could hardly be construed as a direct warning of the atomic bomb and was not taken as such by anyone who did not know the bomb had been created. A technical demonstration of the bomb's power may well have been unfeasible, but certainly a far more definite warning could have been given; and it is hard to believe that a target objective in Japan with but sparse population could not have been found. The truth is we did not try; we gave no specific warning. There were almost two months before our scheduled invasion of Kyushu, in which American ingenuity could have found ways to bring home to the Japanese the impossibility of their position and the horrors of the weapon being held over them; yet we rushed to use the bomb as soon as unconditional surrender was rejected. Had we devised some demonstration or given a more specific warning than the Potsdam ultimatum, and had the Japanese still persisted in continued resistance after some weeks of our psychological offensive, we should perhaps have been justified in the bomb's use; at least, our hands would have been more clean.

But, in fact, our only warning to a Japan already militarily defeated, and in a hopeless situation, was the Potsdam demand for unconditional surrender issued on July 26, when we knew Japanese surrender attempts had started. Yet when the Japanese surrender was negotiated about two weeks later, after the bomb was dropped, our unconditional surrender demand was made conditional and we agreed, as Stimson had originally proposed we should do, to continuation of the Emperor upon his imperial throne.

We were, therefore, twice guilty. We dropped the bomb at a time when Japan already was negotiating for an end of the war but before those negotiations could come to fruition. We demanded unconditional surrender, then dropped the bomb and accepted conditional surrender, a sequence which indicates pretty clearly that the Japanese would have surrendered, even if the bomb had not been dropped, had the Potsdam Declaration included our promise to permit the Emperor to remain on his imperial throne.

What we now know of the condition of Japan, and of the days preceding her final surrender on Aug. 15, verifies these conclusions. It is clear, in retrospect, (and was understood by some, notably Admiral Leahy, at the time) that Japan was militarily on her last legs. Yet our intelligence estimates greatly overstated her strength.

The background for surrender had been sketched in fully, well before the bombs were dropped, and the Strategic Bombing Survey declares that "interrogation of the highest Japanese officials, following V-J Day, indicated that Japan would have surrendered . . . even . . . if the atomic bombs had not been dropped."[71] "Even before the large-scale bombing of Japan was initiated, the raw material base of Japanese industry was effectively undermined. An accelerated decline of armament production was inevitable."[72]

Admiral Chester W. Nimitz, in a talk to the National Geographic Society on January 25, 1946, declared, "I am convinced that the complete impunity with which the Pacific Fleet pounded Japan at point-blank range was the decisive factor in forcing the Japanese to ask the Russians to approach us for peace proposals in July.

"Meanwhile, aircraft from our new fields in the Okinawa group were daily shuttling back and forth over Kyushu and Shokoku and B-29's of the Twentieth Air Force were fire-bombing major Japanese cities. The pace and the fury were mounting and the government of Japan, as its official spokesmen have now admitted, were looking for a way to end the war. At this point the Potsdam Ultimatum was delivered and the Japanese knew their choice.

"They were debating that choice when the atomic bomb fell on Hiroshima. They were debating that choice when our ships shelled installations within less than 100 miles of Tokyo. . . .

"The atomic bomb merely hastened a process already reaching an inevitable conclusion. . . ."

There can be no doubt that this conclusion of Admiral Nimitz will be the verdict of history. Militarily, we "killed" Japan in many different ways: by crushing defeats at sea and on land; by the strangulation of the blockade of which the principal instrument was the submarine; by bombing with conventional bombs. After the seizure of Okinawa—probably even before that—the blockade alone could have defeated Japan; was, indeed, defeating her. Admiral Leahy was right; invasion was not necessary.

By the time "intensive strategic bombing" of the home islands began in March, 1945, production of military supplies in Japan "was already 20 per cent below its peak." And this drop reached 50 per cent by July, 1945. Lack of steel and other minerals, and the inherent industrial weakness of Japan relative to her enemies, doomed the Japs. Japan was just too weak for the war she waged; her ambitions exceeded her capacity.

"Aircraft production from 1942 on (long before either blockade or bombing had become effective) never reached a level sufficient to allow the Japanese to obtain air superiority in any of the contested areas. . . .

"Production of weapons and ammunition for ground troops was not sufficient to keep line troops supplied, to fill the long sea lines, and to maintain adequate stocks in reserve. . . .

"Motor vehicles were never in sufficient supply. . . ."[73]

In the words of a well known Japanese correspondent, Masuo Kato, who was in Washington for the Domei News Agency when the war started: "The thunderous arrival of the first atomic bomb at Hiroshima was only a *coup de grâce* for an empire already struggling in particularly agonizing death throes. The world's newest and most devastating of weapons had floated out of the summer sky to destroy a city at a stroke, but its arrival had small effect on the outcome of the war between Japan and the United Nations."[74]

It is therefore clear today—and was clear to many even as early as the spring of 1945—that the military defeat of Japan was certain; the atomic bomb was not needed.

But if the bomb did not procure victory, did it hasten it?

This question cannot be answered with equal precision, particularly since the full story of the Japanese surrender attempts has not been compiled. But a brief chronology of known events indicates that the atomic bomb may have shortened the war by a few days—not more.

The day before Christmas, 1944 (two months *before* the Yalta conference), U. S. intelligence authorities in Washington received a report from a confidential agent in Japan that a peace party was emerging and that the Koiso cabinet would soon be succeeded by a cabinet headed by Admiral Baron Suzuki who would initiate surrender proceedings.[75]

The Koiso cabinet *was* succeeded by a new government headed by Suzuki in early April, 1945, but even prior to this significant change, the Japanese—in February, 1945—had approached the Russians with a request that they act as intermediary in arranging a peace with the Western powers. The Russian Ambassador, Malik, in Tokyo, was the channel of the approach. The Russians, however, set their price of mediation so high that the Japanese temporarily dropped the matter. The United States was not officially informed of this approach until after the end of the war.

Prior to, coincident with, and after this February attempt, ill-defined peace approaches were made through the Japanese Ambassadors in Stockholm and Moscow, particularly Moscow. These approaches were so informal, and to some extent represented to such a degree the personal initiative of the two Ambassadors concerned, that they never came to a head.

But after a meeting with Stalin in Moscow on May 27, before the trial A-bomb was even tested in New Mexico, Harry Hopkins cabled President Truman that:

"1. Japan is doomed and the Japanese know it.

"2. Peace feelers are being put out by certain elements in Japan. . . ."[76]

In April, 1945, as the United States was establishing a foothold on Okinawa, the Russians in effect denounced their neutrality agreement with Japan, and from then until July 12, the new cabinet was moving rapidly toward surrender attempts.

On July 12, fourteen days before we issued the Potsdam Proclamation, these attempts reached a clearly defined point. Prince Konoye was received by the Emperor on that day and ordered to Moscow as a peace plenipotentiary to "secure peace at any price."[77] On July 13, Moscow was notified officially by the Japanese foreign office that the "Emperor was desirous of peace."[78]

It was hoped that Moscow would inform the United States and Britain at the Potsdam conference of Japan's desire to discuss peace. But instead of an answer from the "Big Three," Ambassador Sato in Moscow was told by Molotov on August 8 of Russia's entry into the war against Japan, effective immediately.

However, since early May—well before this disappointing denouement to the most definite peace attempts the Japanese had yet made—the six-man Supreme War Direction Council in Japan had been discussing peace. On June 20, the Emperor told the (Supreme War Direction) Council that it "was necessary to have a plan to close the war at once as well as a plan to defend the home islands."[79]

The Council was deadlocked three to three, and Premier Suzuki, to break the deadlock, had decided to summon a Gozenkaigi (a meeting of "Elder Statesmen," summoned only in hours of crises) at which the Emperor himself could make the decision for peace or further war. Suzuki knew his Emperor's mind; Hirohito had been convinced for some weeks that peace was the only answer to Japan's ordeal.

The first atomic bomb was dropped on Hiroshima on August 6; Russia entered the war on August 8; and the second atomic bomb was dropped on Nagasaki on August 9. The dropping of the first bomb, and the Russian entry into the war, gave Suzuki additional arguments for again putting the issue before the Supreme War Direction Council, and, on August 9, he won their approval for the Gozenkaigi. But neither the people of Japan nor their leaders were as impressed with the atomic bomb as were we. The public did not know until after the war what had happened to Hiroshima; and even so, they had endured fire raids against Tokyo which had caused more casualties than the atomic bomb and had devastated a greater area than that destroyed at Hiroshima. The Supreme War Direction Council was initially told that a fragment of the Hiroshima bomb indicated that it was made in Germany (!), that it appeared to be a conventional explosive of great power, and that there was only one bomb available. When the Gozenkaigi actually was held on August 14, five days after the second bomb was dropped, War Minister Anami and the chiefs of the Army and Navy General Staff—three members of the War Council who had been adamant for continuation of the war—were still in favor of continuing it; those who had wanted peace still wanted it. In other words, the bomb changed no opinions; the Emperor himself, who had already favored peace, broke the deadlock.

"If nobody else has any opinion to express," Hirohito said, "we would express our own. We demand

that you will agree to it. We see only one way left
for Japan to save herself. That is the reason we have
made this determination to endure the unendurable
and suffer the insufferable."[80]

In the words of Harry F. Kern, managing editor of
Newsweek, who had made a special study, with the
assistance of *Newsweek* correspondents, of the events
surrounding the Japanese surrender:

"I think it's fair to say that the principal effect of
the atom bomb on the Japanese surrender was to provide Suzuki with the immediate excuse for setting in
motion the chain of events which resulted in the surrender." (An "excuse" was necessary—as the attempted military coup, following the Gozenkaigi of
August 14, showed—if the leaders of the "peace
party" were to avoid assassination at the hands of the
rabid militarists of the "war party.")

"However, I think it is also a reasonable surmise
that the Russian declaration of war would have served
the same purpose, and that the dropping of the bomb
was therefore unnecessary. In no case was the dropping of the bomb the reason for the Japanese surrender, and I don't think we can say that it acted as
anything more than a catalyst in advancing the plans
of Suzuki and his supporters."[81]

Or, as the Strategic Bombing Survey puts it, "it is
the Survey's opinion that certainly prior to December

31, 1945, and in all probability prior to November 1, 1945, Japan would have surrendered even if the atomic bombs had not been dropped, even if Russia had not entered the war, and even if no invasion had been planned or contemplated."[82]

This seems, in the light of history, a reasonable judgment, and, in view of our available intelligence estimates, one that we could have then made. It is quite possible that the atomic bombs shortened the war by a day, a week, or a month or two—not more.

But at what a price! For whether or not the atomic bomb hastened victory, it is quite clear it has not won the peace.

Some may point to the comparative tranquility of Japan under MacArthur in the postwar period as due in part to the terror of American arms created by the bomb. This is scarcely so; Japan's seeming tranquility is a surface one which has been furthered by a single occupation authority and the nature of the Japanese people. But I venture to estimate that those who suffered at Hiroshima and Nagasaki will never forget it, and that we sowed there a whirlwind of hate which we shall someday reap.

In estimating the effect of the use of the bomb upon the peace, we must remember, first, that we used the bomb for one purpose, and one only: not to secure a more equable peace, but to hasten victory. By using the bomb we have become identified, rightfully or wrongly, as inheritors of the mantle of Genghis Khan and all those of past history who have justified the use of utter ruthlessness in war.

It may well be argued, of course, that war—least of all modern war—knows no humanity, no rules, and no limitations, and that death by the atomic bomb is no worse than death by fire bombs or high explosives or gas or flame throwers. It is, of course, true that the atomic bomb is no worse qualitatively than other lethal weapons; it is merely quantitatively more powerful; other weapons cause death in fearful ways; the atomic bomb caused more deaths. We already had utilized fire raids, mass bombardment of cities, and flame throwers in the name of expediency and victory prior to August 6, even though many of our people had recoiled from such practices.

Even as late as June 1, 1945, Stimson "had sternly questioned his Air Forces leader, wanting to know whether the apparently indiscriminate bombings of Tokyo were absolutely necessary. Perhaps, as he [Stimson] later said, he was misled by the constant talk of 'precision bombing,' but he had believed that even air power could be limited in its use by the old concept of 'legitimate military targets.' Now in the conflagration bombings by massed B-29's, he was permitting a kind of total war he had always hated, and in recommending the use of the atomic bomb he was implicitly confessing that there could be no significant limits to the horror of modern war."[83]

If we accept this confession—that there can be no limits set to modern war—we must also accept the bitter inheritance of Genghis Khan and the mantles of all the other ruthless despoilers of the past.

In reality, we took up where these great conquerors left off long before we dropped the atomic bomb. Americans, in their own eyes, are a naively idealistic people, with none of the crass ruthlessness so often exhibited by other nations. Yet in the eyes of others our record is very far from clean, nor can objective history palliate it. Rarely have we been found on the side of restricting horror; too often we have failed to support the feeble hands of those who would limit war. We did not ratify the Hague convention of 1899, outlawing the use of dumdum (expanding) bullets in war. We never ratified the Geneva Protocol of 1925, outlawing the use of biological agents and gas in war. At the time the war in the Pacific ended, pressure for the use of gas against Japanese island positions had reached the open discussion stage, and rationalization was leading surely to justification, an expedient justification since we had air superiority and the means to deluge the enemy with gas, while he had no similar way to reply. We condemned the Japanese for their alleged use of biological agents against the Chinese, yet in July and August, 1945, a shipload of U. S. biological agents for use in destruction of the Japanese rice crop was en route to the Marianas. And even before the war, our fundamental theory of air war, like the Trenchard school of Britain, coincided, or stemmed from, the Douchet doctrine of destructiveness: the bombardment of enemy cities and peoples.

Yet surely these methods—particularly the extension of unrestricted warfare to enemy civilians—defeated any peace aims we might have had, and had little appreciable effect in hastening military victory. For in any totalitarian state, the leaders rather than the peoples must be convinced of defeat, and the indiscriminate use of mass or area weapons, like biological agents and the atomic bomb, strike at the people, not the rulers. We cannot succeed, therefore, by such methods, in drawing that fine line between ruler and ruled that ought to be drawn in every war; we cannot hasten military victory by slaughtering the led; such methods only serve to bind the led closer to their leaders. Moreover, unrestricted warfare can never lay the groundwork for a more stable peace. Its heritage may be the salt-sown fields of Carthage, or the rubble and ruin of a Berlin or Tokyo or Hiroshima; but neither economically nor psychologically can unrestricted warfare—atomic warfare or biological warfare—lead anywhere save to eventual disaster.

During the last conflict we brought new horror to the meaning of war; the ruins of Germany and Japan, the flame-scarred tissues of the war-wounded attest our efficiency. And on August 6, 1945, that blinding flash above Hiroshima wrote a climax to an era of American expediency. On that date we joined the list of those who had introduced new and horrible weapons for the extermination of man; we joined the Germans who had first utilized gas, the Japanese with their biological agents, the Huns and the Mongols who had made destruction a fine art.

It is my contention that in the eyes of the world the atomic bomb has cost us dearly; we have lost morally; we no longer are the world's moral leader as in the days of the Wilsonian Fourteen Points. It is my contention that the unlimited destruction caused by our unlimited methods of waging war has caused us heavy economic losses in the forms of American tax subsidies to Germany and Japan. It is my contention that unrestricted warfare and unlimited aims cost us politically the winning of the peace.

But it is not only—and perhaps not chiefly—in public opinion or in the public pocketbook or even in public stability that we have suffered, but in our own souls. The American public is tending to accept the nefarious doctrine that the ends justify the means, the doctrine of exigency. What we have done to ourselves

—and Hiroshima and Nagasaki were heavy blows to a weakening moral structure—can best be expressed in the words of the following editorial from the Bulletin of the Atomic Scientists:

In the first World War, American public opinion was shocked by the sinking of passenger-carrying ships by German submarines; in the second World War, American submarines sank all Japanese ships on sight, and even the revelation that one of these ships was carrying American prisoners of war, has brought no belated wave of indignation at home. The Germans began the terror bombing of cities. The American propaganda long stuck to the pretense that we bombed only "military objectives" (with "pin-point" accuracy). Probably, this was done out of consideration for public opinion; but this concern proved to be excessive. Public opinion in America as well as elsewhere has long since accepted terror bombing of whole cities as legitimate means of warfare. So conditioned, it was able to "take" the news of the destruction of Hiroshima and Nagasaki almost without qualms. Is it not legitimate to predict that if another war comes, no public indignation will meet an announcement of a successful use of psitaccosis virus, or of the wiping-out of enemy crops by chemicals, or poisoning of drinking water in the enemy's capital by radioactive poisons?

In mass fire and bomb raids on German and Japanese cities, America has won the leadership in this form of terror warfare; in the atomic bombardment of Hiroshima (arranged so as to inflict the maximum number of civilian casualties), we have compounded the terror of aerial war a thousandfold.[84]

The use of the atomic bomb, therefore, cost us dearly; we are now branded with the mark of the beast. Its use may have hastened victory—though by very little—but it has cost us in peace the pre-eminent moral position we once occupied. Japan's economic troubles are in some degree the result of unnecessary devastation. We have embarked upon Total War with a vengeance; we have done our best to make it far more total. If we do not soon reverse this trend, if we do not cast about for means to limit and control war, if we do not abandon the doctrine of expediency, of unconditional surrender, of total victory, we shall someday ourselves become the victims of our own theories and practices.

Such mistakes as those outlined in these pages—the attempt to find total victory, to inflict absolute destruction, to use unlimited means, and to mistake military victory for political victory—have been heretofore in history the peculiar characteristics of totalitarian or dictator-led states. The long view, the greatest good of the greatest number, a desire for world tranquilization and peace, have never characterized absolute rulers.

One reflection from a prison cell by the German General Kleist ought to be emblazoned above every doorway in the Pentagon and in the State Department:

"The German mistake was to think that a military success would solve political problems. Indeed, under the Nazis we tended to reverse Clausewitz's dictum, and to regard peace as a continuation of war."[85]

NOTES AND BIBLIOGRAPHY

1. E. H. Wyndam, "The Military Situation in Europe," *The Army Quarterly*, October, 1948

2. William C. Bullitt, "How We Won the War and Lost the Peace," *Life*, August 30, 1948

3. William L. Langer, "Political Problems of a Coalition," *Foreign Affairs*, October, 1947

4. Henry L. Stimson and McGeorge Bundy, *On Active Service* (New York, Harper & Brothers, 1948), p. 414

5. Bullitt, *op. cit.*

6. Langer, *op. cit.*

7. Wallace Carroll, *Persuade or Perish* (Boston, Houghton Mifflin Company, 1948), p. 316

8. Robert E. Sherwood, *Roosevelt and Hopkins* (New York, Harper & Brothers, 1948), p. 903

9. Carroll, *op. cit.*, p. 324

10. Langer, *op. cit.*

11. Harry C. Butcher, *My Three Years with Eisenhower* (New York, Simon and Schuster, 1946), p. 386, 518

12. Elliott Roosevelt, *As He Saw It* (New York, Duell, Sloan & Pearce, 1946), p. 117

13. *The New York Times*, July 22, 1949

14. *Ibid*, November 18, 1949

15. B. H. Liddell Hart, *London Sunday Pictorial*, December 7, 1947, p. 11

16. Albrecht von Kessel, in the German Foreign Office, was "on the fringes" of the anti-Hitler conspiracy in Germany. His diary is quoted in *Germany's Underground* by Allen Welsh Dulles (New York: The Macmillan Company, 1947).

17. Dulles, *ibid*.

18. *The New York Times*, July 25, 1949

19. Hart, *op. cit*.

20. Stimson, *op. cit*., p. 436

21. *Ibid*, p. 437

22. *Ibid*, p. 447

23. Joseph W. Stilwell, *The Stilwell Papers* (New York, William Sloane Associates, 1948), p. 20

24. Stimson, *op. cit*., p. 419

25. Ernest J. King, "The Joint Chiefs of Staff Organization, World War II," Navy Department pamphlet, p. 22

26. Martin Sommers, "Why Russia Got the Drop on Us," *Saturday Evening Post*, February 8, 1947

27. Stimson, *op. cit*., p. 425

28. King, *op. cit*., p. 23

29. Roosevelt, *op. cit*., p. 93

30. In the fall of 1943, according to postwar testimony by German military leaders, Nazi troops in France and the Lowlands numbered 1,370,000 men.

31. King, *op. cit*., p. 35

32. Name known to author but withheld.

33. John R. Deane, *The Strange Alliance* (New York, Viking Press, 1947), p. 43

34. Roosevelt, *op. cit.*, p. 215

35. Reported to author by a participant whose name is known to author but withheld. Eaker, of course, was quite right from the air point of view, but a Balkan invasion offered definite difficulties from the land and naval viewpoints. The Adriatic was not a "healthy place" for ships.

36. Thomas North, "Through the Balkan Underbelly," *The Infantry Journal*, May, 1948

37. Dwight D. Eisenhower, *Crusade in Europe* (New York, Doubleday and Company, 1948), p. 399

38. James F. Byrnes, *Speaking Frankly* (New York, Harper & Brothers, 1947). The background of these decisions has been amplified by Mr. Byrnes in a speech.

39. George S. Patton, Jr., *War as I Knew It* (Boston, Houghton Mifflin, 1947), p. 327

40. Stimson, *op. cit.*, p. 395

41. Frederick C. Sherman, *Combat Command* (New York, E. P. Dutton, 1950), pp. 41, 42

42. King, *op. cit.*

43. Louis Morton, "American and Allied Strategy in the Far East," *Military Review*, December, 1949, p. 38. Abridgement of a chapter from the forthcoming book, *The Fall of the Philippines*

44. King, *op. cit.*

45. *Ibid.*

46. Wesley Frank Craven and James Lea Cate, Editors for Office of Air Force History, *The Army Air Forces in World War II—Volume I* (University of Chicago Press, 1948), p. 184

47. Morton, *op. cit.*, pp. 38, 39

48. *Ibid.*, p. 39

49. King, *op. cit.*

50. L. H. Brereton, "The Brereton Diaries," New York, 1946

51. Douglas MacArthur, in a statement to the press, *The New York Times*, September 27, 1946

52. Craven, *op. cit.*, p. 207

53. Stimson, *op. cit.*, pp. 397, 398

54. *Ibid.*, p. 400

55. Morton, *op. cit.*, p. 27

56. Stimson, *op. cit.*, p. 637

57. Sherwood, *op. cit.*, p. 792. It was his "understanding" that Roosevelt had discussed this proposal a few days earlier with Chiang Kai-shek and had secured his agreement.

58. Stimson, *op. cit.*, pp. 619 ff.

59. Ellis M. Zacharias, "The Inside Story of Yalta," *United Nations World*, January, 1949. Supports independent conclusions to the same end reached by the author.

60. Ija Kawabe, "Interrogations of Japanese Officials, Vol. II," Naval Analysis Division, U. S. Strategic Bombing Survey, Government Printing Office, Washington, D. C., p. 425

61. *Washington Post*, September 9, 1948, Editorial

62. Deane, *op. cit.*, pp. 223ff.

63. *Ibid.*, pp. 240ff.

64. *Ibid.*, p. 249

65. *Ibid.*, p. 263

66. The Kurile Islands agreement was made privately among the "Big Three" without the knowledge—until

weeks afterwards—of Roosevelt's principal advisers or of the British Cabinet.

67. Sherwood, *op. cit.*, p. 867

68. "United States Relations with China," Department of State, Government Printing Office, Washington, D. C., 1949

69. Stimson, *op. cit.*, p. 610

70. *Ibid.*

71. "Air Campaigns of the Pacific War," Strategic Bombing Survey, Government Printing Office, Washington, D. C., 1947, p. 53

72. "The Effects of Strategic Bombing on Japan's War Economy, Appendix A B C," Strategic Bombing Survey, Government Printing Office, Washington, D. C., 1946

73. "Japanese War Production Industries," Strategic Bombing Survey, Government Printing Office, Washington, D. C., 1946, pp. 1, 61

74. Masuo Kato, *The Lost War* (New York, Alfred A. Knopf, 1946)

75. Ellis M. Zacharias, "The A Bomb Was Not Needed," *United Nations World*, August, 1949

76. Sherwood, *op. cit.*, p. 903

77. "The Summary Report on the Pacific War," Strategic Bombing Survey, Government Printing Office, Washington, D. C., 1946, p. 26. *See also* "Japan's Struggle to End the War," same source.

78. Kato, *op. cit.*

79. *Ibid.*, p. 26, *n.*

80. *Ibid.*

81. From a letter to the author, January 5, 1949

82. Strategic Bombing Survey. "The Summary Report on the Pacific War" *op. cit.*, p. 26.

83. Stimson, *op. cit.*, pp. 632-33

84. *Bulletin of the Atomic Scientists*, September, 1948, p. 259

85. B. H. Liddell Hart, *The German Generals Talk*, (New York, William Morrow, 1948), p. 194

In addition to the publications and sources cited in the notes, other works I have consulted include: *Roosevelt and the Russians—The Yalta Conference*, by Edward R. Stettinius, Jr. (Doubleday, 1949); numerous official military histories and monographs; the war reports of General Eisenhower and of General Marshall, General Arnold and Admiral King; and *The Nightmare of American Foreign Policy*, by Edgar Ansell Mowrer (Knopf, 1948)